Building a Firm Foundation

Building a Firm FOUNDATION

An Invitation to Parents of Children
Preparing for Sacraments

Marylynn D. Wesson, D.Min.

OSV

Our Sunday Visitor
Huntington, Indiana

Nihil Obstat
Msgr. Michael Heintz, Ph.D.
Censor Librorum

Imprimatur
✠ Kevin C. Rhoades
Bishop of Fort Wayne-South Bend
August 15, 2022

The *Nihil Obstat* and *Imprimatur* are official declarations that a book is free from doctrinal or moral error. It is not implied that those who have granted the *Nihil Obstat* and *Imprimatur* agree with the contents, opinions, or statements expressed.

28 27 26 25 24 23 1 2 3 4 5 6 7 8 9

Our Sunday Visitor Publishing Division
Our Sunday Visitor, Inc.
200 Noll Plaza
Huntington, IN 46750
www.osv.com
1-800-348-2440

ISBN: 978-1-68192-973-6 (Inventory No. T2708)
1. RELIGION—Christian Ministry—Adult.
2. RELIGION—Christian Ministry—Evangelism.
3. RELIGION—Christianity—Catholic.

eISBN: 978-1-68192-974-3
LCCN: 2022944673

Cover design and interior design: Amanda Falk
Cover art: AdobeStock
Interior art: AdobeStock unless otherwise noted

Printed in the United States of America

To the Abiding Presence
for making everything possible.

Contents

Dear Catechist,

Thank you for saying "yes" to one of the most important experiences you've ever agreed to take on as a catechist. This program is an evangelization process designed specifically for parents, guardians, and other caregivers whose children are preparing for their first sacraments. If you execute this program as designed, you will have the opportunity to personally make a transformational impact on families, the fruits of which will be realized over many generations.

If that seems daunting — well, it is. And while you might not be able to awaken every parent, if even one family benefits from your efforts, your time will have been well spent.

Through the power of prayer, I have confidence that you can accomplish what the Holy Spirit is calling you to do. Every disciple of Jesus Christ is called to evangelize by word, witness, and action. This program provides the words, but it needs catechists like you to be witnesses and to take the actions needed for implementation. So, thank you — the Church needs and is grateful for *you*!

Ad majórem Dei glóriam
For the greater glory of God,
Marylynn Wesson, D.Min.

Introduction

GENERAL ASSUMPTIONS

- ❏ Parents love and want what is best for their children.
- ❏ Identifying as Catholic is no guarantee that a person is evangelized.

GUIDING PRINCIPLES

Relationship: The primary principle and theme of this entire program is relationship. Specifically, the program addresses the importance of having a personal relationship with Jesus and his Church. The closer the relationship is with both, the greater the likelihood that other relationships — family, friends, acquaintances, and even strangers — will be as they should, according to God's will.

Evangelization: Evangelization is the proclamation of the Gospel of Jesus Christ. The Gospel proclaims God's love and the hope of salvation because of Jesus' redemptive acts. The purpose of evangelization is to share this Good News in such a way that, in faith, people will experience a conversion and make an intentional, conscious decision to follow Jesus and become his disciple. This individual faith response is the work of the Holy Spirit.

Conversion: Through the power of the Holy Spirit, conversion begins in the mind, changes the heart, and culminates with a response of turning away from a life of sin to a new life in Jesus Christ. Conversion involves becoming more Christ-like and being open to the transforming power of the Holy Spirit, who continuously converts us to a mature faith as followers of Jesus each day of our lives.

Awareness: Awareness means that we are aware of the significance and impact of the mystery of Christ's redemption of humanity, which offers us the hope of salvation. Full awareness impacts every aspect of our lives as Christians and evokes gratitude and change. Leading parents specifically to becoming aware of their important and primary role as their child's first teacher will help them live all aspects of Christ's redemption in their lives, so that their family can grow together in faith in an intentional way.

OVERVIEW

Building a Firm Foundation (BFF) is an eight-week evangelization and formation process specifically designed for parents whose children are preparing for their sacraments. It is *not* an intergenerational or integrated family catechesis program. Those programs are useful, but implementing them without proper preparation can be premature and unwise. It would be like expecting a child to excel in high school without a sound primary education.

In focusing on the message of the kerygma rather than on specific Catholic doctrine, BFF is a precursor to integrated family programs. This foundational program is designed specifically for parents to start at the very beginning, and it aims to equip them as they — in partnership with their children's catechists — help their children prepare for their sacraments. (For the purposes of this program, "parents" includes guardians and other primary caregivers for children.)

BFF has two purposes: eliciting conversion and inviting a commitment to follow Jesus Christ — to become his disciples. For parents, who are their children's first educators, the program's goal is to stoke their desire to grow together in faith in an intentional way as a family by awakening (or reawakening) parents to the importance of a relationship with Jesus. The program proclaims the kerygma, the initial gospel proclamation that introduces someone to Christ, and it reintroduces parents to the three persons of the Trinity.

If this all sounds familiar — it is. The specific topics covered in BFF are based upon and mirror the essential areas of first evangelization as described in the Period of Evangelization and Precatechumenate in the *Rite of Christian Initiation of Adults*:

- Evangelization by proclamation of the *kerygma* and an appeal for conversion (RCIA, no. 36, 15)
- Awakened faith and conversion as a result of evangelization (RCIA, no. 37, 15)
- Initial formation through "a suitable explanation of the Gospel," and "help and attention so that with a purified and clearer intention they may cooperate with God's grace," with "opportunities … for them to meet families and other groups of Christians" (RCIA, no. 38, 15)
- Further formation designed to encourage a spiritual life of faith, conversion, prayer, and repentance, and to awaken the desire to enter into and deepen a relationship with God through Christ and his Church (RCIA, no. 42, 17)

Although you are not journeying with RCIA catechumen in this program, as a catechist you are helping parents who might be at a similar stage of spiritual development. Based on current research data from both religious and secular sources — such as the Center for Applied Research in the Apostolate (CARA), the Barna Group, and the Pew Research Center — we need to adjust our assumptions that parents are knowledgeable about what it means to be a Christian, let alone what it means to be Catholic. What we can assume, however, is that you will be working in a fertile evangelization field where the "harvest is plentiful" (Mt 9:37). And that's the exciting part of evangelization! The Holy Spirit provides you with numerous occasions to impact the faith formation and development of parents and their families, the rewards of which will be reaped for generations.

I don't want to mislead you to think that evangelizing is easy. It's not — read both the Old and New Testaments for stories that illustrate how frustrating evangelization can be. However, I also don't want to discourage you from taking on the sacred duty of evangelization that is incumbent on all Christians. As a catechist, you might never see the full impact of your service to Jesus' Church in your lifetime. But we know that everything we do in his name is done through the power of the Holy Spirit, who works within God's timeline, not ours. Just know that *everything* you do to actively engage in evangelization will make a positive impact on those with whom you have the privilege of sharing the Good News.

THE NEED FOR A NEW APPROACH

Before we dive into the particulars of the program, an explanation is warranted to show why we need a new approach for evangelizing parents. For more than fifty years, the Church has become increasingly concerned about the challenges and disillusionments parents face — both in society and from the Church herself, especially among younger generations of Catholics. According to the research done by University of Notre Dame sociologist Christian Smith, sociological and cultural shifts, ecclesial changes and scandals, financial and employment pressures, changes in family structure, and — recently — the pandemic are just a few of the issues that have negatively impacted the faith formation of all ages.[1] These issues have created challenges that many parents must resolve in maintaining and sustaining religious participation and commitment.

We see the impact of these issues in the fact that, during the same time frame, Catholic participation and commitment have declined. A 2015 Pew Research Center report reveals that today's young Catholic parents are less religious than were their parents and grandparents. Among all American Catholics, 41 percent no longer identify as Catholic. Of the 59 percent who still identify as Catholic, only 17 percent are from today's generation of young Catholic parents.[2] According to theologian Fr. Thomas Rausch, one of the Church's greatest contemporary challenges is how to retain younger Catholics, whose diminished participation and commitment raise serious questions about the future for them in particular and the American Church in general.[3]

We see other notable changes within today's Catholic families with children of sacramental age, compared with previous generations. According to research data by Mark Gray of the Center for Applied Research in the Apostolate (CARA), most of today's Catholic families (68 percent) have not enrolled their children in either a Catholic school or a parish-based religious education program. Given the historical and current trajectory, today's Catholic children are likely to enter adulthood with less formal, Catholic Church-based religious education than their parents or grandparents received. This likelihood is of great concern: Without parents who are committed to fulfilling their baptismal obligation to raise their children as Catholics, the Church cannot and will not grow, and children will suffer spiritually.[4] Meanwhile, for those Catholic parents who have enrolled their children in either a Catholic school or a parish-based religious education program, the question of how to help them understand the seriousness of their role in their children's faith and spiritual formation becomes all the more important.

The Second Vatican Council document *Lumen Gentium* identifies parents as the "first heralds of the faith"[5] to their children. Yet evidence — both research-based and anecdotal — indicates that parents are increasingly ill-equipped to take on this role. Besides the aforementioned challenges, a large factor contributing to this problem is parents' lack of basic evangelization in the Christian faith. According to Fr. Michael Gallagher, SJ, today's parents represent "a whole new generation of baptized adults whose formative experiences with religion or Church are so thin as to be almost non-existent."[6] This means that baptized Catholic parents are typically not evangelized or sufficiently catechized, both of which are prerequisites to their becoming the "first heralds of the faith" to their children. Author Sherry Weddell maintains that, to the extent that many baptized Catholics have a relationship with the Church, they have been sacramentalized and catechized to a degree, but have yet to be converted through an "explicit, personal attachment to Christ — personal discipleship," by which she means "normative Catholicism as taught by the apostles and reiterated throughout Church history by popes, councils, and the saints of the Church."[7]

Evangelization, then, is the foundational issue that needs immediate attention. While both evangelization and catechesis need attention, they are not in competition. The relationship between the two is organic. For catechesis to be received as intended, evangelization must first occur. But exactly what does this mean and look like? Pope Francis, in *The Joy of the Gospel,* writes about joy — a joy that flows "from the infinite love of God, who has revealed himself to us in Jesus Christ."[8] This is what an evangelized person feels: joy. It's a joy that springs from a personal encounter and a relationship with Jesus. Such a relationship possesses, as Paul wrote to the Philippians, "the peace of God, which surpasses all understanding" (4:7). Only once they are evangelized will parents be more receptive to the catechesis that will nourish and deepen their faith for their entire lives, bringing them to a greater awareness of the holiness and sacredness of their family.

Pope St. John Paul II, called "the pope of the family," addressed the situation of the catechized but not evangelized in his apostolic exhortation *Catechesi Tradendae*. He described baptized Christians who are "still without any explicit personal attachment to Jesus Christ; they only have the *capacity* to believe placed within them by Baptism and the presence of the Holy Spirit."[9] People who have been baptized but have not been sufficiently evangelized and catechized are sacramentally incorporated into the Body of Christ, the Church — but they lack understanding of their new identity, which Romans 6:3 describes as being "baptized into Christ." They know a certain amount about Jesus from the Church's teaching, but they lack a personal familiarity and relationship with him.

Sadly, among parishes, this reality is often not recognized or addressed. The prevalent pastoral assumption is that individuals receive the grace that the sacrament confers — even though serious defects appear to exist in intention, preparation, and understanding. As Sacred Heart Major Seminary professor Ralph Martin observes, the hope is that "the sacrament will take care of it" and that the sacrament alone will lead to the new life it signifies.[10] This hope is faulty. The sacraments only "bear fruit in those who receive them with the required disposition."[11]

As I heard a deacon once explain to RCIA catechumens, the sacraments are not ritual magic. Yet if you ask any DRE, anecdotal evidence suggests that many baptized Catholics perceive the sacraments in exactly this way. As a catechist and as a director of discipleship formation, I am saddened whenever I encounter parents whose attitude about the faith formation of their child is that the sacrament is something that they can "get." That is, they are entrusting their child to parish catechists so that their child can "get their sacraments." And they assume that we can magically turn them into Catholic Christians in the process.

This program — while not offering a complete remedy for this misconception and misunderstanding — addresses the need to awaken in parents the capacity of an active, relational faith inherent in their baptism.

ISSUES THAT IMPACT MANY CATHOLICS' RELIGIOUS WORLDVIEW

Before you implement BFF — before you attempt this process of evangelization — let's review relevant issues that impact many Catholics' religious worldview. Understanding how parents might see reality is the first step in evangelization, as it allows you to meet parents where they are so you can gain their trust. And their perception of reality needs to be taken seriously, not dismissed or derided. Certain issues have heavily influenced *everyone* at this time in history. The hope is that parents will be receptive to the messages of evangelization that, along with eventual catechesis, will enable them to become the first heralds of the Faith to their children.

We need to ponder four primary issues so we can adequately understand their impact on contemporary parents' worldview.

1. **Sacramentalization:** For generations, parochial catechetical programs have focused their efforts on preparing children to receive the sacraments. As Sherry Weddell discovered in her research, an unintended consequence of this sacramentalization focus — one that parents themselves have experienced — is the failure in many instances *to invite ongoing conversion* by awakening a relationship with the Lord through a process of evangelization.[12]
2. **Outsourcing:** Unchallenged and unwittingly perpetuated in many parishes is the mindset that parishes are the sole resource center for the faith formation of children — rather than a partner and resource for training and assisting parents to assume their proper responsibility as first preachers of the Faith. Adding to this challenge, as catechetical leader and author Tom Quinlan found, is that unlike earlier gen-

erations — whose faith was supported and nurtured by the family, the community, and the culture — the formation our children now receive through a parish school or faith formation program is often not reinforced in the home and conflicts with popular culture.[13] Acknowledging this reality, Pope Francis called parents to "return from their exile" and assume their proper role as the first educators of their children, rather than outsource this critical responsibility to the parish.[14]

3. **Secularization:** According to philosopher Charles Taylor, secularization is understood in three ways: (a) public places have "been emptied of God, or any reference to the ultimate reality"; (b) religious belief and practice have declined; and (c) society has moved from an unchallenged belief in God to merely an optional belief in God.[15] Sound familiar? Avery Cardinal Dulles observed that, increasingly, the idea of a distant God, if one exists at all, is common thought. "Many people have lost the sense of God and are drawn into a kind of hedonism that renders them almost impervious to the message of the Gospel."[16] John Paul II's teaching included recognizing that secularization has negatively impacted the "core values of family and life."[17] He countered this impact with his vigorous defense of the family and life, which are threatened today in many ways.
4. **Consumerism:** We touched upon this previously in regard to "getting the sacraments." The influence of consumer culture is significant. Because of this influence, many increasingly view religious beliefs and practices as commodities that can be chosen, passed over, consumed, and discarded for any number of reasons. Driven by market laws, a consumer mentality treats everything, including religion, as a product, according to Avery Cardinal Dulles.[18] You might have heard the term "cafeteria Catholics." Sadly, there's truth behind that term. Parishes unwittingly cater to this mentality when they strive to meet the demands of those who come to church expecting to receive a product, and expecting the ordained and lay leadership to provide it, according to Fr. Robert Rivers, CSP.[19] Concerned that consumerism breeds subjectivism and supports hedonism, John Paul II wrote in *Centesimus annus*: "People are ensnared in a web of false and superficial gratifications."[20] Parents with this mentality transmit an implicit message that their children are likely to imitate as they pick and choose between the teachings of Jesus and the apostles.

Now that we have examined why a new approach is needed, my hope and prayer is that you will understand this program as a response to the situation outlined above. If you have arrived at a greater understanding, then you will also conclude — as did I, after reading the research and papal documents — that we have an urgent need to evangelize parents who do bring their children for religious education and sacramental preparation. We must address the issues by introducing (or reintroducing) parents to the meaningfulness of an encounter and personal relationship with Jesus Christ.

INTENTIONAL EVANGELIZATION CAN MAKE INTENTIONAL DISCIPLES

"Go therefore and make disciples of all nations, baptizing them in the name of the Father and of the Son and of the Holy Spirit, and teaching them to obey everything that I have commanded you. And remember, I am with you always, to the end of the age."

Matthew 28:19–20

According to Saint Matthew, after Jesus' resurrection and before his ascension, Jesus gave his remaining eleven apostles their mission and purpose — and by extension, the mission and purpose of the entire Church. Our

Lord provided a simple three-point process to accomplish this:

1. Make disciples (evangelize)
2. Baptize
3. Teach (catechize)

The first point in this process — the step with which we are specifically concerned in this program — is to evangelize in order to make disciples. Among other things, evangelization involves journeying with someone who has little to no understanding of what it means to have a mature Christian faith.

An intimidating word to many, "evangelization" is often believed to be best left to professional missionaries. However, evangelization isn't and wasn't meant to be complicated or intimidating. Even so, few Catholics know how to evangelize; they have no experience or training in how to personally share with others their faith in Jesus and how to be his disciple. Regardless of their state in life or vocation, they often find the thought of doing so uncomfortable. Yet the reality is that if you are a baptized disciple of Jesus, you *are* a missionary. Pope Francis explains this beautifully in *The Joy of the Gospel*: "Every Christian is a missionary to the extent that he or she has encountered the love of God in Christ Jesus."[21]

Prior generations of missionaries who were sent to foreign lands used the mission *ad gentes* (meaning "to the nations") model of evangelization and catechesis as they ministered in areas of the world where people had little or no knowledge of Jesus. Long ago, Western Europe and later the United States were mission *ad gentes* fields for the Church, and then both regions ceased to need this approach for a long time. However, sadly, both have become mission fields again, calling for a different approach. John Paul II identified the need for a fresh approach to addressing this problem when he called *all* of the faithful to a "New Evangelization."[22]

The influence of secularization (as described above) cannot be stressed enough. It is one of the most challenging considerations in carrying out the New Evangelization. The secularization of society has influenced academia and religious thought to such a degree that both feature an ever-increasing indifference to God and outright rejection of religious belief. Adding to this is the rise of religious relativism, in which even Christians view all religions as equally good. This secularization creates an atmosphere resistant to evangelization, whether it be mission *ad gentes* style or "new."

One way we can respond to this challenge is by preparing people to receive the message of the Gospel — called "pre-evangelization." Session 1 of BFF, "The Big Questions of Life," pre-evangelizes participants by addressing common points of reference and concern among all people. As the Second Vatican Council promulgated in *Gaudium et Spes*, some of those common points are, "The joys and the hopes, the griefs and the anxieties of the men of this age … these are the joys and hopes, the griefs and anxieties of the followers of Christ."[23] By addressing those points of commonality, we can open minds and hearts to the messages of the Gospel and the New Evangelization.

> Once pre-evangelization occurs, then according to the US Conference of Catholic Bishops, the New Evangelization calls each of us to deepen our faith, believe in the gospel message and go forth to proclaim the Gospel. The focus of the New Evangelization calls all Catholics to be evangelized and then go forth to evangelize. In a special way, the New Evangelization is focused on "re-proposing" the Gospel to those who have experienced a crisis of faith. Pope Benedict XVI called for the re-proposing of the Gospel "to those regions awaiting the first evangelization and to those regions where the roots of Christianity are deep but who have experienced a serious crisis of faith due to secularization." The New Evangelization invites each Catholic to renew their relationship with Jesus Christ and his Church.[24]

Today, the RCIA pre-catechumenate uses the same model of evangelization that was used by missionaries of old. The pre-catechumenate is the period in the RCIA process that is dedicated to the proclamation of the Gospel and to conversion. BFF is modeled after this process. It also answers the call for a New Evangelization by reproposing the Gospel with another nuanced goal alongside conversion — namely, awakening. This awakening is intended to bring parents to an awareness of the importance of the Gospel, draw them into a personal relationship with Jesus, and lead them to conversion so that they will willingly commit to becoming his disciples.

Evangelization, then, is intentional. It intentionally introduces people to what is involved in having a personal relationship with Jesus, so that they might choose to become and live as missionary disciples. Evangelization, like conversion, is lifelong and ongoing, and it applies to all the baptized. Once we have attracted followers to the message of the Gospel as revealed in the word of God, then our task becomes helping them to understand and internalize the message, eliciting their conversion and a desire to get to know Jesus better. Conversion is more deeply realized upon participation in the sacramental life of the Church, conforming one's life and will to Jesus and living life as a disciple of Christ.

But make no mistake: No one person has the ability to evangelize, awaken, and convert another by their own power. That process is solely the work of the Holy Spirit, and we are but the flawed human messengers. Those of us who are lay evangelists need to be particularly careful about being preachy. Leave the preaching to the priests and deacons! The job of a lay evangelizer is only to proclaim, witness, lead, direct, and accompany people no matter where they are on their faith journey.

We can find it disheartening to realize how many parents' understanding of faith is no different from that which missionaries in non-Christian countries have long encountered, as research bears out. That is the challenge; that is where intentional evangelization is necessary. The message must be compelling enough so that parents will listen, care, and be open to ongoing conversion of both intellect and heart. All people — not just parents — have to be given the reasons to believe and understand that Jesus Christ truly is Lord and Savior. Only when this happens will people willingly commit and surrender their lives to faith in Christ, trusting in and desiring a close relationship with him. Those freely made individual choices are what make an intentional disciple.

WHAT A PERSONAL RELATIONSHIP WITH JESUS CHRIST LOOKS LIKE

To the Catholic ear, the term "personal relationship with Jesus Christ" often makes the hearer bristle, thinking it sounds too much like evangelical Protestantism — that in a Catholic setting this term is somehow appropriating or venturing into Protestant theology. Nothing could be further from the truth.

The concept of a personal relationship with Jesus is found throughout the Scriptures, beginning in the Old Testament commandment to "love the Lord your God with all your heart, and with all your soul, and with all your might" (Dt 6:5). Jesus repeats this command throughout the New Testament, especially in the Gospels of Matthew, Mark, and Luke. The concept is also found in Church Tradition — specifically the *Catechism of the Catholic Church* and papal teachings.

Claiming, wanting, desiring to have a relationship with Jesus — these are all personal responses of faith. However, that personal response is not a simple "Jesus and me" relationship. It must be a relationship with both Jesus and his Church, one that includes the fullness of Church teaching. As the *Catechism* teaches, the seeds that lead to a personal response of faith begin with baptism within a community of believers: "Baptism is the sacrament of faith. But faith needs the community of believers. It is only within the faith of the Church that each of the faithful can believe. The faith required for Baptism is not a perfect and mature faith, but a beginning that is called to develop. The catechumen or the godparent is asked: 'What do you ask of God's Church?' The response is: 'Faith!'" (1253).

Further, at its beginning, the *Catechism* describes the kind of relationship wanted by God: "At every time and in every place, God draws close to man. He calls man to seek him, to know him, to love him with all his strength. He calls together all men … into the unity of the family, the Church" (1).

Having a personal relationship with Jesus Christ therefore must involve both Jesus and his Church — the Body of Christ — for "a perfect and mature faith" to develop. And for this relationship to take hold and flourish, one must submit to being conformed to Jesus Christ and his Church, as the *Catechism* also teaches: "By faith, man completely submits his intellect and his will to God. With his whole being man gives his assent to God the revealer. Sacred Scripture calls this human response to God, the author of revelation, 'the obedience of faith'" (143).

One of the key words in this passage from the *Catechism* is "submits." The idea of submission is not a popular one, and it often receives pushback — particularly within contemporary Western churches — even though the ultimate act of submission is modeled exactly by what Jesus did for each of us on the cross. It is what all Christians are called to do and what we pray in the Our Father: "Thy will be done."

If someone does not fully accept or comprehend what the Church teaches about a relationship with Jesus and his Church, he or she might understandably ask, "What does a personal relationship 'look like'?" I once heard this question asked by a lay campus minister with two master's degrees, who had been a parish director of religious education. She asked it at a meeting held by the head of evangelization for a religious order that was attended by other campus ministers and directors of religious education. By her own admission, this campus minister *didn't know*. I was at once saddened and surprised. It was not my place to answer her question, but if it had been, this is how I would have responded:

> *A personal relationship with Jesus first begins with an encounter and then an invitation. Through prayer, invite Jesus to come into your heart and take control of your life because, as a sinner, you need him. Only by submitting your will, your life, your heart, and your intellect to him can his will be done in and through you. And just like any other close, personal relationship, one with Jesus involves time: time spent in prayer and adoration, time spent in reading and pondering Scripture, and time spent in listening for the "still, small voice" of the Holy Spirit.*

My response mirrors Pope Benedict XVI's poetic response given at an audience in 2008:

> We are only Christians if we encounter Christ. Of course, he does not show himself to us in this overwhelming, luminous way, as he did to Paul to make him the apostle to all peoples. But we too can encounter Christ in reading sacred Scripture, in prayer, in the liturgical life of the Church. We can touch Christ's heart and feel him touching ours. Only in this personal relationship with Christ, only in this encounter with the Risen One do we truly become Christians."[25]

And he said something similar at an audience in 2009: "Faith is first and foremost a personal, intimate encounter with Jesus, it is having an experience of his closeness, his friendship and his love. It is in this way that we learn to know him ever better, to love him and to follow him more and more. May this happen to each one of us!"[26]

We all are called and invited to the intimate encounter with Jesus of which Pope Benedict spoke — a close, intimate, personal relationship. For Catholics, the sacraments draw us even closer to Jesus through our participation in the Church's liturgical life, which reaches its summit in the Eucharist. Jesus' gift of the Eucharist is the most intimate of encounters and the culmination of the relationship he desires with us. Because of his love for us, besides the gifts of his body and blood, he also gave us the gift of forgiveness as he hung on the cross, the gifts of redemption and the hope of salvation upon his resurrection, and the gift of eternal intercession upon his ascension into heaven. For our part, if we call ourselves his disciples, we must receive and intentionally, freely choose these gifts and the close relationship with Jesus for all of our life.

So there is nothing specifically Protestant about having a personal relationship with Jesus Christ, and Catholics need not be hesitant about using that language. The Church has been using such language since long before the Protestant Reformation. As evidenced by recent papal writings, the Church has not forsaken the language and, in fact, encourages us to embrace it:

- "Only in this personal relationship with Christ, only in this encounter with the Risen One do we truly become Christians." (Pope Benedict XVI)[27]
- "Being a Christian means having a living relationship with the person of Jesus; it means putting on Christ, being conformed to him." (Pope Francis)[28]

As catechists and evangelizers, let us bravely reclaim the term "personal relationship with Jesus Christ," as we work to fulfill the mission of the Church by leading others into an intimate relationship with Jesus and his Church.

WHAT'S AT STAKE

Simply stated: What's at stake is the salvation of souls — eternal life. People become uncomfortable talking about salvation, because they don't wish to seem judgmental. But salvation is the ultimate goal of any evangelization effort. Salvation is specifically what Jesus came to do, as we recite in the Nicene Creed: "for us men and for our salvation he came down from heaven." However, somewhere along the way, society in general (and many people in particular) developed a very different perspective of what salvation involves. This section explains the surprising — but prevalent — understanding today.

In the early 2000s, University of Notre Dame sociologists Christian Smith and Melissa Denton conducted a unique research project to better understand American adolescents' religious and spiritual lives. The study participants are now the grownup versions of that demographic; many are now married with children. Smith and Denton's research found that the dominant religious worldview of many young people entailed beliefs in several moral statutes not exclusive to any of the major world religions. Their worldview was not a new religion or theology; rather it was a set of commonly held spiritual beliefs. Smith and Denton termed this de facto religious creed Moralistic Therapeutic Deism (MTD), and it includes these tenets:[29]

- A God exists who created and orders the world and watches over human life on earth.
- God wants people to be good, nice, and fair to each other, as taught in the Bible and by world religions.
- The central goal of life is to be happy and to feel good about oneself.
- God does not need to be particularly involved in one's life except when he is needed to resolve a problem.
- Good people go to heaven when they die.

MTD's core creedal components include the following:

- **A moralistic approach to life:** Feeling good about oneself is essential to living a moral life. It means being nice, kind, pleasant, respectful, and responsible; working on self-improvement; taking care of one's health; and doing one's best to be successful.[30]
- **Therapeutic benefits:** Attaining subjective well-being by resolving problems and getting along with people will make one feel good, happy, secure, and at peace. MTD is "about providing therapeutic benefits to its adherent" as opposed to the more traditional notions of "repentance from sin, of keeping the Sabbath, of living as a servant of a sovereign divine, of steadfastly saying one's prayers, of faithfully observing high holy days, and of building character through suffering."[31]
- **Belief in a particular kind of God:** God exists, created the world, defines our general moral order, and keeps a safe distance. MTD's God is not particularly or personally involved in human affairs — especially affairs in which one would prefer not to have God involved. The remoteness of God, in this view, implies that he is "something like a combination Divine Butler and Cosmic Therapist: he's always on call, takes care of any problems that arise, professionally helps his people to feel better about themselves, and does not become too personally involved in the process."[32]

Smith and Denton did not find that MTD was an alternative religion among youthful adherents. Rather, they concluded that MTD is "colonizing" many established religious traditions and congregations in the United States with elements of this "creed," assimilated by degrees, "converting believers in the old faiths to its alternative religious vision of divinely underwritten personal happiness and interpersonal niceness."[33] As one admittedly agnostic parent — who was also a baptized Catholic — told me, "I think that as long as you are a good person, if there is a heaven, you'll go there when you die." But this alternative religious worldview is not limited to younger adults. Smith and Denton concluded that this belief system is widespread among many older adults as well, indicating that the young people in the study were absorbing and reflecting religiously what the adult world was modeling and inculcating. They found this "creed" to be particularly evident among mainline Protestants and, sadly, Catholics.

The danger of this religious creed is that it often leads its adherents away from the Church — and away from a relationship with Jesus that would culminate in their salvation. Scripture scholar Dr. Michael Barber defines salvation as "being changed in Christ — being truly remade."[34] We are essentially being saved from being un-Christ-like. Salvation is about past, present, and future transformation;[35] each person participates in salvation to the degree that he or she responds to God's love and will as Jesus did. Neither the Church nor Jesus are necessary for salvation from the MTD perspective. MTD leads people to subjectively determine which spiritual or religious principles to live by, rather than to seek to live according to God's will for their lives.

Although no person can judge whether any soul is saved — that's not our job, it's Jesus' job — it *is* our responsibility to witness to, proclaim, and teach the Gospel. As Jesus taught in the Parable of the Lamp (Mk 4:21–25), we are called to be a light for others — a light that enlightens and leads them to God. By the power of the Holy Spirit, we must courageously shine our light so that it attracts others to Jesus for their souls' sake.

THE HOPE

Keep in mind this assumption: Parents love and want what is best for their children. Our responsibility is to help parents understand that what is best for everyone is a relationship with Jesus, so that they can spend eternity with him. BFF is an effort toward the evangelizing opportunity presented to the Church, because it offers a parent formation program that prepares parents for the foundational Good News of Jesus Christ — the *kerygma* — using a methodology that John Paul II called an "evangelizing catechesis."[36]

To that end, this program was designed to invite conversion and draw parents into a desire for a deeper faith by focusing on the significance of a personal relationship with Jesus Christ and his Church, the importance of the word of God, the power of prayer, and the blessings of participation in a faith community.

The Church has an exciting evangelizing opportunity at this time in history — a domestic mission field. It cannot and should not discount or ignore this opportunity. This chance occurs when parents voluntarily bring their children for sacrament preparation, because the reception of their sacraments becomes a priority for them as their children come of age. Before and beyond the time of preparation, parents should also prioritize transmitting faith to their children to fulfill their missional duty as baptized members of the Body of Christ and as their children's first faith educators.

The Church's responsibility to parents, therefore, is to support their decision to bring their children for their sacrament preparation by offering the parents themselves a formation that awakens them to the importance of their role as first educators in the transmission of faith throughout the entirety of their children's lives. This responsibility is more fully realized when parents themselves have been evangelized. The question then becomes this: How does the Church evangelize the evangelizers, the baptized who live in Christian families?

Attempts to awaken parents through an evangelization process must begin by recognizing that they have embraced modern culture. Embracing current secular culture perpetuates the four main problems outlined above, and we must consider these problems when we evangelize parents: (1) a sacramentalization focus; (2) the parish being treated as the sole resource for a child's faith formation; (3) a general secularization of society; and (4) a consumer mentality that views religious practices and beliefs as commodities. The challenge for the Church is how to effectively address these issues, which have contributed to the currently low levels of religiosity and involvement that impact the transmission of faith within Catholic families.

This program responds to the specific, identified contemporary challenges facing the Church by addressing parents whose children are preparing for their sacraments. It assists them in fulfilling their roles as their children's first teachers of the Faith, with the goal of igniting their desire to grow together in faith with their children in an intentional way. The hope is that BFF will awaken parents to the importance of their role as the first heralds of the Gospel of Jesus — the family evangelizers — for their children.

The Church can assist by providing families with

the grace and resources necessary to be evangelizers. Hearts, minds, lives, and families can be changed by the accompanying grace of God. As Pope Francis has taught, parents who have a relationship with Jesus and his Church are better equipped to introduce their children to the beauty of the Catholic Faith and can help cultivate an attraction to or desire for a relationship with Christ, because of their love for their child and the witness of their lives.[37] When children see their parents committed to Jesus and the Church, they are much more likely to be committed themselves.

HOW TO USE THIS PROGRAM

Running the Program

Through trial and error, I discovered certain things that helped the program run successfully. The research and groundwork have been completed, tested, and refined, so I encourage you to take and use these suggestions.

Enthusiasm and Joy: People are attracted to enthusiastic, joyful people. Getting an audience's attention isn't difficult if you truly believe in and are passionate and excited about the subject matter you're sharing. When it comes to evangelizing, the most important thing to consider is that you cannot give or share that which you do not have. What does this mean? If you're going to conduct this program, you should be a joyful disciple of Jesus who understands and has a personal relationship with him.

Backing of the Pastor: Ideally, you will have 100 percent support from the parish pastor. If he's skeptical, he won't be as willing to defend the program should he receive any pushback or complaints from parents for being required to participate in it as part of sacramental preparation. If he grants you permission to offer this program but is lukewarm about the idea, do it anyway. The Holy Spirit is ultimately in charge and will clear the way for you if necessary.

The Question of Fees: If at all possible, don't charge a fee for the program. No costs should be associated with it that can't be absorbed into the fee charged for the children. (In my perfect world, I wouldn't charge a fee for children either. But parish budgets usually don't allow for that, and old habits die hard.)

Required Participation: Make parents' participation in the program a required component of their child's preparation to receive their sacraments. If your parish has a website that describes children's faith formation offerings, and you are using *Building a Firm Foundation* for parent formation, be sure to revise the information on your website to reflect this new program for parents. Also, full disclosure of the program requirement during registration will evoke better cooperation from parents, so clear communication is key. Here is suggested content:

Website Announcement

Because [church's name] views faith formation as a total parish experience, we are offering a unique program for parents, guardians, and other caregivers of children preparing for the reception of first sacraments (reconciliation and the Eucharist) or confirmation, or of children enrolled in the RCIA adapted for children, as a required component of their child's formation and preparation. The class will be held during your child's class for the first eight weeks. [Include registration directions/information.]

Email (if you follow up registration with a welcome or acknowledgment email)

Dear Parent or Guardian,

We are so happy that you registered your child in our faith formation class to prepare them to receive their first sacraments. [For confirmation only: We are so happy that you registered your child in our confirmation preparation program.] We are honored and blessed that you have chosen us to partner with you in this preparation.

Because [parish name] views faith formation as a total parish experience, a required component of your child's formation and preparation is your attendance at an eight-week faith formation program called Building a Firm Foundation. We will meet in [provide location] on [dates and time], during the same time as your child's class.

[Add any other pertinent details.]

[Add registration details.]

Please contact me should you have any questions. We look forward to seeing you soon!

Scheduling: Each session should run concurrently with a session of the children's sacramental preparation program. Therefore, the exact start time and duration of each parent session should mirror those of the children's program, so that parents have time to deliver their child to sacramental preparation class, attend Building a Firm Foundation, and then end in time to retrieve their child.

- *Duration.* The more time you can allot to both sessions (parent and child), the better. But seventy-five minutes is ideal, to allow sufficient time for all portions of each session. This length might mean tweaking the children's sessions to match, but the extra time with the parents — and children — is worth the tweak. Anything less than sixty minutes is not recommended at all.
- *Sunday Classes.* If at all possible, schedule and conduct sacramental preparation classes on Sunday mornings between Masses. (In fact, all children's classes should ideally be held on Sunday mornings.) Such an arrangement makes it easier for participants to go to Mass with their families before or after the program. One of the biggest frustrations among catechists is the fact that many children's families do not attend Mass *at all.* The children attend classes during the week but then do not attend Mass on Sundays. Catechists on social media religious education groups suggest making Mass attendance a requirement — especially for children preparing for their first sacraments — and ask families either to attest to their attendance or provide proof (like a bulletin signed by the officiant). This arrangement is possible if your pastor understands its importance. In one parish, I worked with the pastor to adjust the Sunday morning Mass times, just a little, to accommodate such a schedule. Two books — *Rebuilt*[38] and *Divine Renovation*[39] — provide justification for such a Sunday schedule. This adjustment provides families with an easy opportunity for Mass attendance and Sunday school to become part of their Sunday morning schedule. It also allows parents to attend adult faith formation programs beyond BFF (if those too are held on Sunday mornings) and/or to volunteer as catechists during this time.

Parent/Guardian Orientation: Hold an orientation for all children's faith formation programs a week or two before classes begin. Include parents and children alike. I cannot overstate how helpful we found this to be. My pilot program held our orientation in the church on a Sunday between Masses and approached it much like a "meet the teacher" night that schools hold. The orientation gives both the children and parents the opportunity to meet the catechist(s) and visit the room(s) where class will be held. Doing so made the actual first day of class go more smoothly than it did during the years before we held orientation, because this time everyone knew exactly where to go and who their catechists were. At the orientation, be sure to have the pastor come to say a few words of welcome and encouragement. This invitation also gives him the opportunity to explain the importance of Mass attendance.

Provide folders — not just sheets of paper — with pertinent information such as the calendar, information about the curriculum, prayer cards, and so on. Your children's curriculum publisher often provides some handouts as well. Yes, you'll have some of that information available online, but many families still appreciate a hard copy of important information. As you know, a class schedule calendar will probably be displayed on the family refrigerator for all members to reference.

Hospitality: Hospitality is important. If at all possible, provide light refreshments at each session. If people volunteer to provide home-baked goodies, that's a bonus. If the program meets on Sunday mornings, another idea is to have a parish organization host a Doughnut Sunday once a month — or even every Sunday — for everyone in the parish, and ask for donations to help defray the cost. The idea of hospitality is to provide an opportunity for people to mingle and visit over food. It's a great community builder.

The Order of Sessions: The program follows a structured format, and each session builds on the previous one. Don't mix up the order; the order is purposeful. The program provides two alternate methods to present each session. One is the scripted presentation in this book; the other is a corresponding PowerPoint with notes that duplicate the scripts. (See the "Resources" section starting on page 91 for information on accessing the PowerPoints and other digital materials.) The PowerPoint, in testing, seems to engage participants better, so I strongly encourage you to use the PowerPoints. Even so, do refer to the scripted presentation in this book for signposting about what to say before and during the PowerPoint presentation.

Intentional Format: The program is a presentation, not a discussion or sermon. This intentional presentation format does not allow questions and answers other than those posed as part of a particular session. It's important to stay on topic. Time is too limited to go off on tangents or to allow the presentation to get off-track with a participant's question. If someone has a specific question, you might offer to stay after class, discuss via email or phone, or make an appointment to meet with him or her separately.

Time Management: The presentation is intended to provide information for participants to reflect on during the small-group discussion segment. Therefore, you need to complete the presentation with plenty of time left for the small-group discussion and closing. Be mindful of the time and don't linger, but don't rush through it either. If you stick closely to the scripted presentation in this book or to the PowerPoint notes, you should have plenty of time for small-group discussion — which, in some ways, is more important.

Small-Group Discussion: When it's time for small-group discussion, that's when you can pass out the session's discussion questions. Don't have them available at the start of the session. If you put them out in advance, participants will review the questions and formulate answers before they hear the presentation. We want them to pay attention to the presentation without distractions. Also, the questions are meant to be surprises, so that the groups will answer spontaneously rather than plan responses.

The Role of Music: Music is mighty in setting the tone and mood. I suggest playing "easy listening" piano or guitar music softly as participants arrive. This instrumental music is to be played during the gathering time and turned off prior to greeting everyone and beginning the session. Music streaming services have several options for inspirational or religious instrumental playlists. (Note that Gregorian chant — while beautiful — sets a somber tone. Aim for inspiring and uplifting contemporary instrumental music instead.) Most sessions have at least one suggestion for recorded music to use for reflection during either the opening or closing. These songs were carefully curated; they are not necessarily hymns (although a few are used in liturgies) and are meant to be listened to, not sung along with. They were chosen for the impact of their lyrics and melody, which may stay longer in someone's thought process than anything they hear during a presentation. These suggestions were chosen to appeal to the heart. Use them if at all possible.

Find some way to project the lyrics for participants to read along while the song plays. This strategy is an effective way to reach adults who are visual learners, not just auditory learners. When I conducted this program, I located and projected online music videos of the songs that display the lyrics to allow the participants to follow along; I avoided videos that did not include the lyrics. Or if you choose to play an MP3 of a given song, you can often find lyrics online and download them to project them on the screen. This approach similarly allows participants to follow along. Either way, showing the lyrics as you play the song seems to make a great impact on participants.

Recommended Take-Home Resources: Recommended take-home handouts are listed for most of the sessions. (For more information on downloading or ordering these handouts, please visit the "Resources" section on page 91.) Put them out during the small-group discussion segment, so that participants can pick them up — if they want to — as they leave. As with the discussion questions, you don't want to put them out before the presentation, because participants may be tempted to read them instead of listening to the presentation. Let the participants decide for themselves whether they want to pick these up as they leave, so don't pass them out either.

Free Bibles and/or Books: This suggestion might be unattainable for many parishes' budgets, but it's still worth proposing. Understanding that most families in the pilot program did not have a Bible at home, we gave every family *The New Catholic Answer Bible*, available from Our Sunday Visitor, at the end of the final session as a gift. This Bible edition is useful specifically for parents, because it has colorful inserts that ask and answer difficult questions about Church teaching that children may very well ask at some point. If you can do this, please don't tell the participants in advance — make a lasting impression and let them be surprised. The looks of delight on the faces of my participants who received the Bibles were like the looks of children opening Christmas gifts.

Our parish was blessed to have a donor offer to buy the Bibles when needed, so we didn't have to budget for them. If you do have it within your parish budget (or can likewise identify a donor) to purchase these Bibles for program participants, then please do so. One way to convince your parish finance council that the Bibles — specifically *The New Catholic Answer Bible* — are needed is to point out that the money is an investment in families' spiritual future. This colorful, attractive Bible is an ongoing, visible reminder of the time spent, and it is a silent but powerful evangelization tool in the home. We were also able to give a copy of OSV's *Encounter with Christ: My Mass Book* to each child preparing for the sacraments. This book is written at a child's level to help them better understand the Mass. Every participant, at every program, was visibly appreciative and touched by both gifts.

If you are able to give a Bible and/or a Mass book to each family, place the item(s) in a gift bag with the family's name on the bag, so one family member can pick it up on the way out. Alternatively, hand out the gift bags. This way you don't have two people from the same family inadvertently picking up two bags.

Session Topics

1. The Big Questions of Life
2. The God of Love and Mercy
3. Who Do You Say That I Am?
4. The Comforter
5. The Good News
6. Faith and Community
7. The Power of Prayer
8. Listening to That Still, Small Voice

Session Structure

As suggested in the "Running the Program" section above, each session should run seventy-five minutes, from the gathering before the official start time through the closing prayer. Some of the sessions are densely packed. But field testing has demonstrated that a seventy-five-minute program can easily stay on schedule if you follow the script, don't digress often (or at all), and don't allow open discussion during the presentation portion.

Because you have a lot of information to convey, you need to begin the sessions on time, right after the time allotted for gathering.

The section headings in the sessions give you target durations for the review, presentation, and small-group discussion. But expect that the time will flow organically within a sixty-minute span. Some weeks you might spend a few extra minutes on the review or presentation and less on small-group discussion. Other weeks, the opposite will occur. Just remember not to linger on the presentation. Using the PowerPoints will help you stay on track and engage participants more effectively.

Finally, be sure to end the session promptly so that you have time for the closing and to release participants to go gather their children from their class.

SCHEDULE	TIME
1. Gathering: sign-in, refreshments, community building	10 minutes before official start time
2. Greeting and introduction	5 minutes
3. Review	10 minutes
4. Opening prayer	3 minutes
5. Presentation	15 minutes
6. Small-group discussion	20 minutes
7. "Today's Takeaway" moment	2 minutes
8. Closing: remarks, announcements, and closing prayer	10 minutes

Supplies and Equipment

- Candle with matches or safety lighter
- Bible
- Crucifix
- White tablecloth
- Music player (smartphone, tablet, computer, CD player with speaker)
- Microphone (optional)
- Podium
- Screen or blank wall
- Projector (if needed)
- Laptop
- MP3 files or playlist of instrumental music to play during gathering time
- MP3 file or internet link to music video, along with lyrics to project for optional opening or closing music
- Round tables seating six to eight persons each, with chairs
- Pencils or pens for each table
- Light refreshments: water, coffee and tea, packaged savory items, or baked goods
- For sessions 1 and 2 only: Whiteboard, chalkboard, easel with large paper pad, or large piece of craft paper taped to a wall

Resources

- Sign-in sheet
- PowerPoint for the session
- Small-group discussion guidelines (table tent)
- Handouts: "Small-Group Discussion" questions for the specific session and "Today's Takeaway" slips (one copy for each participant, plus a few extras)
- Recommended take-home resources for the specific session (one copy for each household, plus a few extras)

Session Setup

Altar Table: Prepare a small, simple altar table with a candle, open Bible, and crucifix. Place a plain white covering on the altar so the items will stand out. Don't clutter the altar with flowers or anything else — we want the focus to be on the imagery and symbolism of those three items. Light the candle before the session begins.

Music: Play soft instrumental piano or guitar music in the background as people arrive to set the mood. Keep the music tracks light and uplifting (As stated earlier, Gregorian chant may be too somber.) Turn off the music when you are ready to begin the session.

Tables: Round tables with six to eight chairs are preferable; if round tables are unavailable, long tables will do. Tables of some kind are necessary to promote community; setting up just chairs is not recommended. Arrange the tables and place the following on each: the table tent of small-group discussion guidelines, pens or pencils, and the "Today's Takeaway" slips. (Hold on to the small-group discussion questions for now, so they won't be a distraction during the presentation. Instead, hand them out when it is time for small-group discussion.)

Hospitality: Hospitality is very important. If at all possible, set up a side table with beverages and light packaged refreshments. Refreshments need not be fancy or expensive, but having them says, "Welcome, we were expecting you and are so glad you are here!" If someone offers to bring something for the next session, graciously accept.

Take-Home Handouts: Designate a table or other space near the point of exit. During small-group discussion time, you can place the recommended take-home resources on this table and invite participants to pick them up when they leave. Let participants decide whether they want them; don't pass them out. (Do not make the resources available as participants arrive, as they might pick them up to read instead of listening to the presentation.)

Session 1

The Big Questions of Life

This beginning session is unique from the other seven in that it is not focused on proclaiming the *kerygma*. Rather, session 1 is preparing participants to receive the gospel message. As a result, this particular session can be considered "pre-evangelization." It addresses what might be required to establish trust and pique participants' interest in hearing a message they may be lukewarm to, may reject outright because they find it irrelevant, or may resist because it is in opposition to how they want to live life. Pre-evangelization is necessary to meet participants where they are in life so that their hearts and minds will open and awaken to the desire to grow closer to Jesus and his Church.

PREPARATION

Objectives

To answer several big questions of life, such as "Does my life have meaning?" and "Who is going to love me?"

To identify the importance of these existential questions and why they are foundational questions for one's entire life.

Handouts

Discussion questions

"Today's Takeaway" slips (cut from the master sheet of three slips in the "Resource" section)

"My Journey" worksheet

Recommended Resources

"What Catholics Need to Know About Making Their Homes a Domestic Church" article

"10 Things That Make for a Great Catholic Family" pamphlet (OSV)

"Living as a Domestic Church" pamphlet (OSV)

SESSION: THE BIG QUESTIONS OF LIFE

Greeting and Introduction (5–8 min.)

- ***Smile***, *turn off the instrumental music, and call the session to order.*
- ***Thank*** *the participants for coming and for prioritizing their child's faith and sacramental formation.*
- ***Ask*** *them politely to silence their phones and refrain from looking at them during the session, barring a family emergency.*
- ***Begin*** *the PowerPoint presentation, if you are using it, by advancing to the "Introduction" slide. Introduce yourself briefly (about one minute). Tell them about yourself, such as your marital/vocation status, profession, education, children and grandchildren, hobbies, etc. You don't need to go into great detail — please do not linger — but you do want to provide enough information so that they begin to relate to you. Provide any contact information that you wish to share.*
- ***Explain*** *what these sessions are about and how they will be presented, in these or similar words:*

These sessions will provide you with an awareness of your critical role in your child's faith formation. The sessions will reacquaint you with the basic tenets of the Christian faith to help you when your children ask questions. The sessions won't involve large-group Q&A, as a rule. Rather, I will be presenting material and information for your consideration and reflection.

We won't have enough time to address specific questions during the presentations. If you have questions that aren't addressed during my presentation or during small-group discussions, please ask me those questions outside class. You can approach me via email, appointment, or an after-session discussion.

My actual presentation is only half of each session. The second half is small-group discussion. This time will be an important opportunity for you to reflect upon and discuss what you've just heard in the presentation.

Preview (1 min.)

Introduce this session in these or similar words:

In this session we're going to look at existential questions that we all ask ourselves; specifically, two big questions of life:

- Does my life have meaning?
- Who is going to love me?

Regardless of what we look like, what we do, our personal preferences, and so on, the one thing that we all share is our common humanity.

Collectively, we are all journeying together during this time in history, in this thing called "life."

Opening Prayer (2–5 min.)

- **Say,** "Let's open with a prayer."
- **Invite** those gathered to make the Sign of the Cross: "In the name of the Father, and of the Son, and of the Holy Spirit."
- **Read** the opening prayer as follows:

Heavenly Father, thank you. Thank you for life. Thank you for everything with which we have been blessed. Thank you for the people we encounter on our life's journey to love, to learn from, and to forgive.

As we gather here today, we pray for your mercy and grace as we begin our individual and collective journeys and are awakened to and informed about how to build the best foundation for our life as well as for those we love.

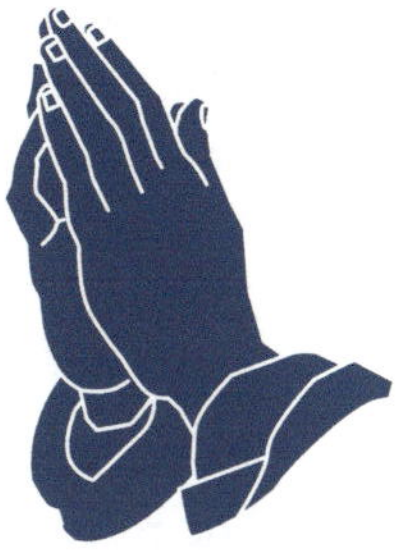

Accompany us, O Lord, along the journey, and please grant us the strength and fortitude to persevere.

We pray this through Christ, our Lord. Amen.

- **Conclude** the prayer with the Sign of the Cross.

Optional opening: Locate an MP3 or internet link for the song "Strength for the Journey," by Michael John Poirier. Try to locate a video of the song that displays the lyrics as they're sung. If you play an MP3 instead, locate the lyrics online and project them for the participants to follow along. Invite the participants in these or similar words: "Let's reflectively — and prayerfully — listen to this song about journeying, before we open in prayer." Play the song for the gathering.

Presentation (20 min.)

Begin the presentation in these or similar words:

The title of this session is "The Big Questions of Life." But I'll bet that you have some initial questions, which we will address today:

- Why do I have to be here?
- What's all this "Building a Firm Foundation" stuff about?

Before I answer those questions, I'd like to ask each of you a question.

Ask the participants, "What do you most desire for your child?" Record answers on the whiteboard, chalkboard, or paper. Leave the answers up for the duration of the session. Tell the group that you will revisit this question near the end of the presentation, when you'll add your own response.

Why Do I Have to Be Here?

Ask the participants this rhetorical question: "Why do you have to be here?" Then answer the question in these or similar words:

You may have been raised a "cradle Catholic," attended Catholic school or college, attended CCD during childhood, and so on. If so, you're naturally curious about the need to attend these sessions as part of your child's sacramental preparation.

[*Name of parish*] views faith formation — particularly sacrament preparation — as a total parish experience. Our mission as catechists, in partnership with you as parents and guardians, is to form and make disciples of the children entrusted to our care as they prepare for the reception of their sacraments.

This parish can only do so much. We aren't even most important in your child's faith formation.

What *is* most important in your child's faith formation is you: their parents. This is because parents are the first educators of faith for their children — what the Church calls the "domestic church."

This program is specifically for parents and guardians whose children are receiving formation and are being prepared for the reception of either their first sacraments (reconciliation and the Eucharist) or confirmation, or who are enrolled in the RCIA adapted for children (baptism, reconciliation, the Eucharist, and confirmation). We want you to become aware of how important your own role is in your children's formation.

You are cojourneyers — as are the catechists and entire parish — with your child as they prepare for their sacrament(s). The journey is ultimately a search for God and is the most intimate quest of our lives. To accompany another person on this intimate search is a privileged journey.

EyePix

OSV file photo/Jim Olvera

When we are witnesses to another's awakening in faith — especially if we are accompanying our children — the experience draws us closer together. It reaffirms our own belief, and it often fills us with awe.

What's All This "Building a Firm Foundation" Stuff About?

Answer this second question in these or similar words:

For the eight sessions that we will be journeying together, we use the metaphor of "building a firm foundation" to describe what we are doing here, applying the metaphor to our faith development.

If our faith isn't firmly and solidly formed and built on the rock that is Jesus, our faith can become compromised — much like a building foundation that has not been properly poured, set, and reinforced.

Existential Questions

Return to the existential questions you posed at the beginning of the presentation. Review them in these or similar words:

> This first session looks at those existential questions that all humans ask themselves at some point in our existence. Your children will ask themselves these questions at some point:
>
> - Does my life have meaning? What is the meaning of life and, specifically, *my* life?
> - Who is going to love me? Who or what is going to fill that empty void that we all feel and experience at some time?
>
> Let's look at each of these in turn.

Does My Life Have Meaning?

Restate the question. Present the material in these or similar words:

Humans have always asked questions about the meaning of life. No other creatures can do this.

Throughout history, people have searched, trying to find satisfying answers to these questions through five means:

- Pondering life's meaning
- Reflecting on personal experience
- Developing relationships with others
- Engaging in exploration and study
- Listening to or reading others' perspectives on the meaning of life

All of these paths to discovery are valid — but they are limited. None of them fully answer everything we need or want to know. We search for something more.

Explain that faith is the answer to these questions:

For me, personally, and for many — if not everyone in this room — that *more* is faith.

Faith is a gift from God and helps us to see our lives and the world through the eyes of God. A person of faith comes to the awareness that there is more to life than can be seen.

Through the eyes of faith, we learn three truths:

- God is near.
- God is closer than we can comprehend.
- God is the source of all life.

Who Is Going to Love Me?

Restate the question. Present the material in these or similar words:

We often feel an emptiness. When we do, we need to fill it with something. Often, we fill that void with things or pursuits that we shouldn't.

We do this because things aren't the way they should be. Not in the world. Not in our neighbors. Not in ourselves. We aren't as kind, as generous, or as loving as we should be. We do things we shouldn't. We can be selfish, arrogant, sometimes even cruel. Sometimes we use other

people for our own ends.

When we allow our lives to take this direction, we are actually living in a "love poverty." We are all looking for love. For our entire life, we thirst for it. The problem is that our search for love never actually, completely delivers what we yearn for.

Living for ourselves in our search, we try to find love through other imperfect human beings, material goods, career success, and so on. None of those things is bad in and of themselves; but ultimately none can fill that emptiness and "love poverty" that we all experience.

Sin can be defined as making choices that result in a "failure in genuine love for God and neighbor" (CCC 1849). When we live this way, sin pushes us into the emptiness of love poverty.

To free ourselves from this poverty, let's consider a few things:

- God created you, loves you, and wants only the best for you. But accepting this is sometimes difficult, because God's best and what we want often conflict.
- God wants to reveal himself — and indeed has revealed himself — to us through Jesus Christ.
- God wants to be at the center of our lives.

One of the best witnesses of someone who lived the will and love of God was Saint Teresa of Calcutta, popularly known as Mother Teresa, who was canonized in 2016. An embodiment of Christ, she was a woman who was rich in love even while she lived and served amid abject, literal poverty. I'm sure you can think of other examples of people who seem to have nothing yet possess everything that is truly important in life.

Small-Group Discussion (18 min.)

Invite the groups to transition to small-group discussion time. Ask the groups at each table to take a minute to review the small-group discussion guidelines on the table tent.

Pass out the "My Journey" worksheet and the discussion questions handout. Explain the activity in these or similar words:

Please review the discussion questions handout. Notice that the first item asks you to complete the "My Journey" worksheet. This worksheet is for your use only — it won't be picked up.

After everyone at your table completes the "My Journey" worksheet, briefly introduce yourself to the others at your table.

Together discuss the questions on the handout you've been given. Answer as many as time allows.

Call everyone's attention back to you after eighteen minutes. Conclude the discussion time in these or similar words:

Let's revisit the question I asked at the beginning: What do you most desire for your child? You had time to consider your private responses earlier, and I said that I would give you my answer to what I most desire for your child.

My answer is this: eternal life with God!

Why? Because I care about your children. They are my brothers and sisters in Christ. I care about what happens to them and their spiritual development. Most of all, I care about introducing them to Jesus and helping them become his disciples.

Please reflect on that this week and on your own initial response to that question. How do they compare?

As the program unfolds, I hope that you come to an understanding of why eternal life in Jesus Christ is the most important thing for all of us to desire for everyone.

Today's Takeaway (1 min.)

Direct the participants' attention to the slips of paper on their tables.

Give the following instructions:

- These slips of paper have a date and a place for you to write down "today's takeaway."
- Please take a minute to write down something that struck you and that you'd like to reflect on or discuss with a friend, a spouse, or another participant.
- Please take this slip home and use it to prompt further reflection or discussion.

Closing (10 min.)

***Smile** and thank everyone for being there and participating. Tell them that you look forward to seeing them next week, when the topic will be "The God of Love and Mercy."*

Make any pertinent announcements. Point out where participants can obtain take-home resources on their way out. Ask anyone who came in late to be sure to sign in before they leave, especially if you are keeping attendance.

- **Say**, "Let's close with a prayer."
- **Invite** those gathered to make the Sign of the Cross: "In the name of the Father, and of the Son, and of the Holy Spirit."
- **Read** the closing prayer as follows:

May the Lord bless you and keep you. May the Lord make his face to shine upon you, and be gracious to you. And may the Lord grant you and yours peace. Amen. (Based on Nm 6:24–26, RSVCE)

- **Conclude** the prayer with the Sign of the Cross. Wish everyone a GREAT week!

Session 2
The God of Love and Mercy

This second session moves away from the pre-evangelization of the first session, which prepared participants to receive the gospel message. This session discusses the existence of God and reintroduces participants to the first Person of the Trinity, God the Father, reminding them of his unending and unconditional love.

PREPARATION

Objective
To reflect upon the nature of God the Father by pondering these questions and statements: "Who is God the Father?" and "The Father's love is unconditional," as well as "The Father's mercy is never-ending."

Handouts
Discussion questions

"Today's Takeaway" slips (cut from the master sheet of three slips in the "Resource" section)

Recommended Resources
"God the Father" pamphlet (OSV)

"Teaching Your Child About God" handout

SESSION: THE GOD OF LOVE AND MERCY

Greeting and Introduction (5 min.)

- ***Smile**, turn off the instrumental music, and call the session to order.*
- ***Thank** the participants for coming back and for prioritizing their child's faith and sacramental formation. Say, "It's good to see everyone!"*
- ***Ask** them politely to silence their phones and refrain from looking at them during the session, barring a family emergency.*
- ***Reintroduce** yourself with your name and any contact information that you wish to share.*
- ***Introduce** the session in these or similar words:*

Last week, we talked about the big questions of life.

This session's topic is about God the Father — the first Person of the Trinity — specifically focusing on his love and mercy. We'll reflect upon God the Father by pondering one question and two statements:

- Who is God the Father?
- The Father's love is unconditional.
- The Father's mercy is never-ending.

First, let's review some things we covered in the previous session.

Review (5–7 min.)

Remind the participants of the previous session, in these or similar words. Begin the PowerPoint presentation, if you are using it:

> At the first session, we considered the metaphor of a building's foundation to describe how our faith should be firmly built upon the "rock" of Jesus. Anything less is a shaky foundation, one that is subject to compromise and even destruction.
>
> We reflected upon and answered some existential questions:

- Does my life have meaning?
- Who is going to love me?

These are existential questions that everyone asks themselves at some point — and your children will too.

We also answered some initial questions that I'm sure many of you had:

Why do I have to be here? Answer: This is a total parish experience that the parish leaders and catechists take very seriously. Faith formation and sacramental preparation are a partnership between parents and the parish.

What is this program all about? Answer: This program specifically caters to parents and guardians whose children are being prepared to receive their sacrament(s). The goal is to help you accompany your children on their faith and sacramental journey.

Who is most important in my child's faith formation? Answer: Everyone your child comes into contact with is important — but in a special and particular way ... YOU and your family!

Remind participants that the family is often called the "domestic Church." Review the following points:

You are the domestic church because you are the most important influence on your child's faith formation and spiritual journey.

The domestic church is the smallest body of gathered believers in Christ. The term dates all the way back to the first century AD — to the earliest Christians.

The domestic church is the first place where we encounter the selfless love of other people.

Remind the participants that you also covered the idea of faith in the previous session. Review the following points:

In addition to asking and answering questions, we also talked about faith:

- Faith is a gift from God.
- Faith helps us to see our lives and the world through the eyes of God.
- A person of faith understands that there is more to life than can be seen.

Through the eyes of faith, we learn three things:

- That God is near
- That God is closer than we can comprehend
- That God is the source of all life

Opening Prayer (2–5 min.)

- **Say**, "Let's open with a prayer."
- **Invite** those gathered to make the Sign of the Cross: "In the name of the Father, and of the Son, and of the Holy Spirit."
- **Read** the opening prayer as follows:

Heavenly Father, as we gather here today, we thank you for the many blessings, graces, and mercies of the past week.

Please open our eyes and our hearts, Lord, so that we may, indeed, see and love like you and grow daily in faith.

We pray this through Christ, our Lord. Amen.

- **Conclude** the prayer with the Sign of the Cross.

Optional opening: Locate an MP3 or internet link for the song "Open My Eyes, Lord," by Jesse Manibusan. Try to locate a video of the song that displays the lyrics as they're sung. If you play an MP3 instead, locate the lyrics online and project them for the participants to follow along. Invite the participants in these or similar words: "Let's reflectively — and prayerfully — listen to this song before we open in prayer." Play the song for the gathering.

Presentation (17 min.)

Begin the presentation in these or similar words:

Our topic this week is God the Father; specifically, his love and mercy.

First, we need to understand that God is Trinity. He is a loving communion of three divine Persons: the Father, the Son, and the Holy Spirit. (We will discuss the Son and the Holy Spirit in the next two sessions.) When we speak of God, we mean the Trinity.

Everyone at some point questions God's existence, especially in certain circumstances:

- During times of trouble
- If we possess a more rational and concrete thought process versus a creative and imaginative mindset (thinking about God can become a right brain versus left brain tension)
- When we reject the idea of God because we don't want anyone or any being telling us what to do or holding us accountable — we want to live life our way, on our own terms

Those who do believe and have great faith still have questions:

- Just who is God?
- How can I know God?
- How can I have a relationship with someone who can't be comprehended with the senses — be touched, seen, or felt?

Many people today especially struggle to have a relationship with God the Father, as he can seem more distant than the Son and the Holy Spirit.

At such times, you can ask the Father to show you who he is — to open your heart and mind — through three strategies: prayer, Scripture, and encounters with other people.

This simple request — to open your heart — just might result in good things:

- New insights as to the nature of God as our loving Father and Father of creation. (Jesus addressed him as "Abba," which in Aramaic is an intimate term that characterizes a loving, personal relationship.)
- Recognition of the times that the Father has been with you
- A new understanding that the Father has always loved you and will always love you unconditionally

Tell the participants that God the Father's love is unconditional. Ask, "What does that mean to you?" Record answers on the whiteboard, chalkboard, or paper. Leave up the answers for the duration of the session.

Continue the presentation in these or similar words:
Scripture tells us that nothing can separate us from God.

As Paul writes to the Romans: "For I am convinced that neither death, nor life, nor angels, nor rulers, nor things present, nor things to come, nor powers, nor height, nor depth, nor anything else in all creation, will be able to separate us from the love of God in Christ Jesus our Lord" (8:38–39).

Ask the participants to reflect quietly for a minute on two questions:

- If you feel a distance, who put that distance between you?
- Who always welcomes you back?

Continue by explaining God's unconditional love, in these or similar words:

God the Father's unconditional love is evidence of his mercy:

- He wants us.
- He constantly searches for us.
- He is always reaching out to us — with arms wide open.

God meets us where we are:

- In the depths of our sorrow
- At the moments of our greatest sins
- At the height of our greatest joys
- In the mundane, everyday aspects of life

Small-Group Discussion (20 min.)

Invite the groups to transition to small-group discussion time. Remind them to review the small-group discussion guidelines on the table tent, as needed.

Pass out the discussion questions handout. Explain the activity in these or similar words:

Please review the discussion questions handout.

Together discuss the questions on the handout you've been given. Answer as many as time allows.

Call everyone's attention back to you after 20 minutes.

Today's Takeaway (1 min.)

Direct the participants' attention to the slips of paper on their tables.

Give the following instructions:

- Please take a minute to write down something that struck you and that you'd like to reflect on or discuss with a friend, a spouse, or another participant.
- Please take this slip home and use it to prompt further reflection or discussion.

Closing (10 min.)

***Smile** and thank everyone for being there and participating. Tell them about the next session in these or similar words:*

Last week, we talked about the big questions of life. This week, we talked about the God of love and mercy.

Next week, we'll answer the question: "Who do you say that I am?"

Make any pertinent announcements. Point out where participants can obtain take-home resources on their way out.

Ask anyone who came in late to be sure to sign in before they leave, especially if you are keeping attendance.

- **Say**, "Let's close with a prayer."
- **Invite** those gathered to make the Sign of the Cross: "In the name of the Father, and of the Son, and of the Holy Spirit."
- **Read** the closing prayer as follows:

  May the Lord bless you and keep you. May the Lord make his face to shine upon you, and be gracious to you. And may the Lord grant you and yours peace. Amen. (based on Numbers 6:24–26, RSVCE)

- **Conclude** the prayer with the Sign of the Cross. Wish everyone a GREAT week!

Session 3
Who Do You Say That I Am?

This second session continues reintroducing the Persons of the Trinity to participants. The presentation focuses on the second Person, God the Son — Jesus Christ. It reminds everyone of Jesus' desire for a personal relationship with us, his disciples. It also explains how and why he came to redeem humanity and offer us the hope of salvation.

PREPARATION

Objectives
To reflect upon the nature of Jesus by pondering and answering these questions: Who do you say that I am? What did Jesus come to do? And why did Jesus die and rise from the dead?

To examine why the death and resurrection of Jesus are historical, life-changing events to believers.

Handouts
Discussion questions

"Today's Takeaway" slips (cut from the master sheet of three slips in the "Resource" section)

Recommended Resources
"Jesus Christ: The Son of God" pamphlet (OSV)

'Teaching Your Child About Jesus" handout

SESSION: WHO DO YOU SAY THAT I AM?

Greeting and Introduction (5 min.)

- ***Smile****, turn off the instrumental music, and call the session to order.*
- ***Thank*** *the participants for coming back and for prioritizing their child's faith and sacramental formation. Say, "It's good to see everyone!"*
- ***Ask*** *them politely to silence their phones and refrain from looking at them during the session, barring a family emergency.*
- ***Introduce*** *the session in these or similar words:*

Last week, we talked about the God of love and mercy.

This session's topic is Jesus' question in Matthew 16:15: "Who do you say that I am?" Jesus asks each of us this question. Please keep this question in mind throughout this session.

We'll reflect upon the nature of Jesus by pondering three additional questions:

- Do we have historical proof for the existence of Jesus?
- What did Jesus come to do?
- Why did Jesus die and rise from the dead?

First, let's review some things we covered in the previous session.

Review (5 min.)

Remind the participants of the previous session, in these or similar words. Begin the PowerPoint presentation, if you are using it:

Last time, we introduced five key ideas about God, and we spent time focusing on God the Father, the first Person of the Trinity:

- God (Father, Son, and Holy Spirit) is the object of our faith.
- Everyone questions the existence of God.
- You can ask God the Father to open your heart and mind to show you who he is: the loving Father of creation and the first Person of the Trinity.
- God's love is unconditional.
- God's love and mercy endure forever.

Transition to opening prayer in these or similar words:

This week, Jesus — the second Person of the Trinity, the Son of God — is the topic. What you hear today will help you be more comfortable talking to your child about him.

Opening Prayer (2 min.)

- **Say**, "Let's open with a prayer."
- **Invite** those gathered to make the Sign of the Cross: "In the name of the Father, and of the Son, and of the Holy Spirit."
- **Read** the opening prayer as follows:

Dearest Lord Jesus, as we gather here today, we thank you for the many blessings, graces, and mercies of the past week. Help us to truly see you as the Son of God.

Please bless our time together today by placing in our hearts the desire to know you more clearly, follow you more nearly, and love you more dearly, so that we will always follow where you lead.

We pray this in your name, Jesus. Amen.[1]

- **Conclude** the prayer with the Sign of the Cross.

Presentation (22 min.)

Begin the presentation in these or similar words:

Our topic this week is Jesus. We will be answering the question that he asks each of us: "Who do you say I am?"

Jesus has been asking everyone that question since his earthly ministry. In Matthew 16:15, we read that Jesus asked his disciples: "But who do you say I am?"

Ask everyone to stop and ponder the following two questions in their heart. Don't invite or record responses — just pause for a few seconds after each question to allow reflection.

How might you answer if Jesus asked you, "Who do you say I am"?

Upon what would you base your answer?

Explain that a person's answer to any of these questions depends on their knowledge of Jesus.

Introduce the three areas for discussion in this presentation:

We will ask — and answer — three related questions:

- Do we have historical proof for the existence of Jesus?
- What did Jesus come to do?
- Why did Jesus die and rise from the dead?

1. The Historical Jesus

Acknowledge that some people question whether Jesus really existed — much like they question the existence of God.

Some of the things in the Bible seem implausible and impossible. What/where is the concrete evidence?

Other than the Bible, is there historical proof of Jesus' existence?

Describe the historical proof of the life of Jesus in these or similar words:

Both pagan and Jewish contemporary accounts either directly or indirectly record and corroborate Jesus' existence, including the accounts of Publius Cornelius Tacitus, Pliny the Younger, Suetonius, and Josephus.

These ancient historians recorded consistent facts from two thousand years ago:

- A man named Jesus came from the town of Nazareth, in what is modern-day Israel.
- He gained a large following as he taught and preached throughout the region.
- During the years he roamed the region, he upset the Jewish religious leaders, who handed him over to the Roman authorities for prosecution.
- The Romans executed him by crucifixion.
- After Jesus' crucifixion, his followers claimed that he had risen from the dead.
- Some people believed this claim and began following those who were preaching it. Those who believed the claim were the earliest members of the Christian church.

This historical evidence was recorded outside of the Bible.

Based on the historical evidence, even skeptics agree on the following facts:

- Jesus actually existed as a historical person.
- He was not a legend, myth, or fictional hero.
- He really lived in the first century AD.
- The New Testament contains the fullest, most reliable record of his life and ministry.

The evidence raises two questions:

- What did Jesus come to do?
- Why did he die and rise from the dead?

2. Jesus' Mission

Explain that Jesus came to fulfill a specific mission.

Jesus came for a specific mission: to die for the sins of humanity, so that we might have the *hope* of salvation and eternal life.

He proved his divinity as the Son of God to his disciples through a life and ministry that was filled with miracles, according to Scripture:

- He was born to a virgin, Mary.
- He walked on water.
- He gave sight to the blind and healed the sick.
- His greatest miracle was his own bodily resurrection following his death on the cross.

According to Scripture, there were many more.

Explain that Jesus' resurrection is the ultimate answer to two important questions about his mission: What

did Jesus come to do? And why did he die and rise from the dead?

Jesus' resurrection is at the center of the Christian faith. Without the resurrection, there is no Christianity.

But the story doesn't end there.

Tell the participants that relationship and discipleship are key to both answers. Continue in these or similar words:

Jesus doesn't want you simply to know about him. Many people know about him and believe he existed but still do not have a relationship with him.

Jesus wants to have a reciprocal, personal relationship with *you*.

Jesus wants *you* to become *his* disciple.

This reality raises two further questions: What does a relationship with Jesus mean? And what does being a disciple look like?

What does a relationship with Jesus mean? Answer: Having a relationship with Jesus is an encounter and an intentional invitation for him to enter your heart as you seek to know, love, trust, and follow him.

What does being a disciple "look" like? Answer: Following Jesus — being his disciple — involves turning to him and away from self and sin. Being a disciple means being continuously transformed and conformed to his will.

Having a relationship with Jesus and being his disciple require an intentional decision on your part to put him — and his will for your life — ahead of anything else that is important to you: career, money, material things, social position, other people, etc. None of these things are necessarily bad, but when they become the center of your world — when you make any of them the most important thing to you — your spiritual life greatly suffers.

Explain relationship and discipleship further, in these or similar words:

Making Jesus the foundation of your life prepares you for your own mission: to do the will of the Lord according to your vocation and calling.

Jesus seeks and loves you with a love that is amazing and beyond comprehension. When he was dying on the cross, *you* were on his mind. He died for you, and he loves you.

To agree intellectually that Jesus Christ is the Son of God and that he died on the cross for our sins is not discipleship. Nor is having a one-time emotional experience.

Trusting Jesus to come into your life to forgive your sins and to transform you into what he wants you to be — that is the key to discipleship.

A relationship with Jesus as his disciple is directly tied to three things:

1. **Our human condition:** Jesus understands. Jesus was sent to earth by God the Father to become human and to redeem humanity.
2. **Our redemption:** Jesus redeemed everyone. Redemption opened the way to heaven and the *hope* of salvation.
3. **Our salvation:** Jesus' death offers everyone the *hope* of salvation. Jesus desires salvation for every single person.

Ask the participants the following questions, and allow them a minute to reflect quietly.

- What is your response to Jesus' desire?
- To be saved, Jesus asks that we repent of our sins and intentionally follow him. Are we ready to do that?

Small-Group Discussion (20 min.)

Invite the groups to transition to small-group discussion time. Remind them to review the small-group discussion guidelines on the table tent, as needed.

Pass out the discussion questions handout. Explain the activity in these or similar words:

Please review the discussion questions handout.

Together, discuss the questions on the handout you've been given. Answer as many as time allows.

Call everyone's attention back to you after twenty minutes.

Today's Takeaway (1 min.)

Direct the participants' attention to the slips of paper on their tables.

Give the following instructions:

- Please take a minute to write down something that struck you and that you'd like to reflect on or discuss with a friend, a spouse, or another participant.
- Please take this slip home and use it to prompt further reflection or discussion.

Closing (10 min.)

***Smile** and thank everyone for being there and participating. Tell them about the next session in these or similar words:*

Last week, we talked about God the Father and his love and mercy. This week we talked about God the Son, exploring Jesus' question "Who do you say that I am?"

Next week, we'll talk about the Comforter.

Make any pertinent announcements. Point out where participants can obtain take-home resources on their way out.

Ask anyone who came in late to be sure to sign in before they leave, especially if you are keeping attendance.

- **Say**, "Let's close with a prayer."
- **Invite** those gathered to make the Sign of the Cross: "In the name of the Father, and of the Son, and of the Holy Spirit."
- **Read** the closing prayer as follows:

  May the Lord bless you and keep you.
  May the Lord make his face to shine upon you, and be gracious to you.
  And may the Lord grant you and yours peace. Amen. (based on Numbers 6:24–26, RSVCE)

- **Conclude** the prayer with the Sign of the Cross. Wish everyone a GREAT week!

Optional closing: Locate an MP3 or internet link for the song "Amazing Love," by Graham Kendrick. Try to locate a video of the song that displays the lyrics as they're sung. If you play an MP3 instead, locate the lyrics online and project them for the participants to follow along. Invite the participants in these or similar words: "Let's reflectively — and prayerfully — listen to this song before we close in prayer." Play the song for the gathering.

Session 4
The Comforter

Finalizing the reintroduction of the Trinity to participants, this session focuses on the third Person: the Holy Spirit. The session reminds everyone of the nature of the Holy Spirit and his role in the life of a believer.

PREPARATION

Objectives
To reflect upon the nature of the Holy Spirit by answering the question, "Who is the Holy Spirit?" as well as to examine the importance of the Holy Spirit in believers' lives.

To examine the Holy Spirit's role in the lives of participants and their families.

Handouts
Discussion questions

"Today's Takeaway" slips (cut from the master sheet of three slips in the "Resource" section)

Recommended Resources
"The Holy Spirit" pamphlet (OSV)

"Teaching Your Child About the Holy Spirit" handout

SESSION: THE COMFORTER

Greeting and Introduction (5 min.)

- ***Smile***, *turn off the instrumental music, and call the session to order.*
- ***Thank*** *the participants for coming back and for prioritizing their child's faith and sacramental formation. Say, "It's good to see everyone!"*
- ***Ask*** *them politely to silence their phones and refrain from looking at them during the session, barring a family emergency.*
- ***Ask*** *for five volunteers to read Scripture passages. Give each a slip of paper with a Bible passage to read when called upon.*
- ***Introduce*** *the session in these or similar words:*

Last week, we talked about Jesus: who he is, what he came to do, and why he rose from the dead.

This session's topic is the Comforter, one of the names of the Holy Spirit, the third Person of the Trinity. We'll reflect upon the nature of the Holy Spirit by pondering and answering two questions:

- Who is the Holy Spirit?
- Why is the Holy Spirit important in our lives?

First, let's review some things we covered in the previous session.

Review (5–7 min.)

Remind the participants of the previous session, in these or similar words. Begin the PowerPoint presentation, if you are using it:

"Who do you say that I am?" is the question Jesus asks of us. This question leads to other questions.

- How would you answer Jesus' question?
- Upon what would you base your answer?
- What did Jesus come to do?
- Why did Jesus die and rise from the dead?

Remind the participants that the Bible, plus historical evidence from outside the Bible, helps us arrive at answers to these questions.

Based on evidence from Roman and Jewish historians, we can state three facts:

- Jesus actually existed.
- He was not a legend, myth, or fictional hero.
- He really lived in the first century, and the New Testament contains the fullest, most reliable record of his life and ministry.

In the New Testament Scriptures, Jesus' full story was recorded by his disciples.

Jesus "proved" his divinity as the Son of God to his disciples through a life and ministry that was filled with miracles.

Point out that the New Testament Scriptures also inform us about Jesus' mission:

Jesus had a specific mission: to die for the sins of humanity.

In fact, without the Resurrection, Christianity is meaningless. Jesus would have been, as author and lay theologian C. S. Lewis posited, either a liar, a lunatic, or Lord, and we would have no hope for eternal life.[1] Without the Resurrection, Christianity is just another cult-like religion, following the teachings of a dead founder.

However, according to the New Testament and other historical sources, Jesus was crucified, died, was buried, and rose on the third day. The Resurrection proves that Jesus is who he said he was — the Son of God — who has conquered the ultimate evil of death.

The Resurrection of Jesus is the most important teaching and truth of Christianity and is the focal point of the New Testament. The Resurrection was the focus of the preaching of the apostles in the Book of Acts.

Ask the participants: "Understanding what Jesus has done for us, is there anything he desires from us?" Answer in these or similar words:

Yes — a relationship!

He desires that we not just know about him, but become his disciples. Being a disciple involves SO much more than just knowledge of him. Knowledge does not equal belief. Think of the people who "know" about Jesus but are not believers, much less disciples.

Transition to opening prayer in these or similar words:

This week, the Holy Spirit is our topic. What you hear today will help you when you talk to your child about the Holy Spirit.

Opening Prayer (2 min.)

- **Say**, "Let's open with a prayer."
- **Invite** those gathered to make the Sign of the Cross: "In the name of the Father, and of the Son, and of the Holy Spirit."
- **Read** the opening prayer as follows:

Oh Holy Spirit, Jesus told us that he would not leave us orphaned and that he would send you to us. Please help us to recognize your presence in all situations as you are the Comforter, never leaving or abandoning us.

You are that Abiding Presence that we can always call upon, if we only would. Help us to learn to turn to you in order to discover and become aware of your presence in every moment of our lives.

We pray this through Christ, our Lord. Amen.

- **Conclude** the prayer with the Sign of the Cross.

Presentation (20 min.)

Begin the presentation in these or similar words.

Our topic this week is God, the Holy Spirit, also known as the Comforter. The Holy Spirit is the third Person of the Trinity.

The Holy Spirit is known by several names: Intercessor or Advocate, Spirit of Truth, Indweller of Believers, Spirit of God, and Paraclete (Greek for counselor). There are many others.

Let's look at and answer two questions:

- Who is the Holy Spirit?
- Why is the Holy Spirit important in our lives?

1. Who Is the Holy Spirit?

Present the material in these or similar words:

To answer this question, we must look at the role of the Holy Spirit in the Trinity.

The first Person of the Trinity is God the Father, the second Person is God the Son (Jesus), and the third Person is God the Holy Spirit.

The Father is God, the Son is God, and the Holy Spirit is God.

But the Father is not the Son or the Spirit. The Son is not the Father or the Spirit. And the Holy Spirit is not the Father or the Son.

God — the Father, the Son, and the Holy Spirit — is a loving communion of Persons.

"The divine persons do not share the one divinity among themselves but each of them is God whole and entire" (CCC 253).

There is only one God, who exists as a triune unity of three Persons that are in relation to one another. "The Father is wholly in the Son and wholly in the Holy Spirit; the Son is wholly in the Father and wholly in the Holy Spirit; the Holy Spirit is wholly in the Father and wholly in the Son" (CCC 255).

The word *Trinity* is not found in the Bible; however, the Trinity was revealed by Jesus.

- **Jesus' Baptism:** "And the Holy Spirit descended upon him in bodily form, as a dove. And a voice came from heaven, 'You are my Son, the Beloved; with you I am well pleased.'" (Lk 3:22)
- **The Last Supper:** "But the Advocate, the Holy Spirit, whom the Father will send in my name, will teach you everything, and remind you all that I have said to you." (Jn 14:26)
- **The Great Commission:** "Go therefore and make disciples of all nations, baptizing them in the name of the Father and of the Son and of the Holy Spirit." (Mt 28:19)

Explain that we encounter the Holy Spirit in several ways:

Introduced in **baptism**: Baptism invokes all three Persons of the Trinity. Through baptism, we receive new life through the power of the Holy Spirit. We receive the *capacity* to live out our baptismal promises.

In the **Eucharist**: The Holy Spirit transforms the bread and wine into our spiritual food of the Lord's body and blood.

At **confirmation**: What began at baptism and is nourished by the Eucharist is completed. All three Persons of the Trinity come upon the confirmandi to strengthen them for life's journey.

- At confirmation, the person being confirmed (the confirmandi) — assuming he is of the age of reason and properly disposed — accepts responsibility for his faith and life in Christ.
- At confirmation, we are asked to make promises, and in return the Holy Spirit makes a promise: to transform us.
- You will be transformed if you are properly disposed and fully participating with the power of the Holy Spirit. The promises we make and receive at confirmation need to be continually renewed and ratified for us to fully experience the Holy Spirit's transforming power.

But baptism, Eucharist, and confirmation aren't the only sacramental encounters. The Holy Spirit is present in all seven sacraments and in other ways. That leads us to the second question.

2. Why Is the Holy Spirit Important in Our Lives?

Explain that when we receive the Holy Spirit, we receive the promises of God.

Ask the five volunteers to read the following five Scripture passages about what God promises to do through the power of the Holy Spirit, when we call upon him.

- Guide us to the truth. (Jn16:13)
- Empower us to be witnesses to Jesus. (Acts 1:8)
- Gather us together as a Christian community. (Acts 2:46–47)
- Pour God's love into our hearts. (Rom 5:5)
- Pray for us when we can't or don't know how. (Rom 8:26)

Continue the presentation after the volunteers read these verses.

The Seven Gifts of the Holy Spirit

Explain that God not only makes us these promises, but that the Holy Spirit gives us gifts.

The seven Gifts of the Holy Spirit are as follows:

1. Wisdom
2. Understanding
3. Counsel
4. Knowledge
5. Piety
6. Fortitude
7. Fear of the Lord

Explain the following points about these gifts of the Holy Spirit:

These gifts are *freely* given — but all gifts are not necessarily given to all equally.

The Sacrament of Confirmation "increases the gifts of the Holy Spirit within us" (CCC 1303). When a confirmed person *cooperates* with the graces and gifts from the Holy Spirit, that person grows spiritually, as they listen and obey his gentle direction.

The Twelve Fruits of the Holy Spirit

Explain that in cooperation with the Holy Spirit, from these gifts, fruit is produced.

The twelve Fruits of the Holy Spirit are as follows:

1. Kindness
2. Generosity
3. Joy
4. Charity
5. Self-control
6. Faithfulness
7. Gentleness
8. Goodness
9. Chastity
10. Peace
11. Patience
12. Modesty

Explain the following points about these fruits of the Holy Spirit:

These fruits result from the process of freely receiving the gifts of the Holy Spirit. The fruits are things that we give back.

The fruits born of the gifts of the Holy Spirit are to be used for the benefit of others and the Church. By the grace of the Holy Spirit, anyone who is confirmed — assuming he or she is properly disposed — is given the capacity to live a righteous and virtuous life according to his or her vocation. This is only possible with a close, personal relationship with Jesus. In the Gospel of John (15:1) Jesus calls himself "the true vine," as he is our anchor to whom we must remain attached in order to bear fruit.

Conclude the presentation in these or similar words to transition to the small-group discussion period:

Wouldn't it be a wonderful world if every confirmed Christian fully received all the gifts of the Holy Spirit and then produced fruit?

We must pray for the outpouring of the Holy Spirit — not only for ourselves but for others, because the Holy Spirit changes our hearts!

Small-Group Discussion (20 min.)

Invite the groups to transition to small-group discussion time. Remind them to review the small-group discussion guidelines on the table tent, as needed.

Pass out the discussion questions handout. Explain the activity in these or similar words:

Please review the discussion questions handout.

Together discuss the questions on the handout you've been given. Answer as many as time allows.

Call everyone's attention back to you after twenty minutes.

Today's Takeaway (1 min.)

Direct the participants' attention to the slips of paper on their tables.

Give the following instructions:

- Please take a minute to write down something that struck you and that you'd like to reflect on or discuss with a friend, a spouse, or another participant.
- Please take this slip home and use it to prompt further reflection or discussion.

Closing (10 min.)

***Smile** and thank everyone for being there and participating. Tell them about the next session in these or similar words:*

Last week, we explored answers to the question "Who do you say that I am?" This week we talked about the Holy Spirit, our Comforter.

Next week, we'll talk about the Good News and why the word of God is essential in the life of a Christian.

Make any pertinent announcements. Point out where participants can obtain take-home resources on their way out.

Ask anyone who came in late to be sure to sign in before they leave, especially if you are keeping attendance.

- **Say**, "Let's close with a prayer."
- **Invite** those gathered to make the Sign of the Cross: "In the name of the Father, and of the Son, and of the Holy Spirit."
- **Read** the closing prayer as follows:

Come, Holy Spirit, fill the hearts of your faithful and kindle in them the fire of your love. Send forth your Spirit, and they shall be created. And you shall renew the face of the earth.

O God, who by the light of the Holy Spirit did instruct the hearts of the faithful, grant that by the same Holy Spirit we may be truly wise and ever enjoy his consolations. Through Christ, Our Lord. Amen.

- **Conclude** the prayer with the Sign of the Cross. Wish everyone a GREAT week!

Optional closing: Locate an MP3 or internet link for one of the following songs: "Holy Spirit Rain Down," by Hillsong Worship; or "Sacred Silence" by Tom Booth, Anthony Kuner, and Jenny Pixler. Try to locate a video of the song that displays the lyrics as they're sung. If you play an MP3 instead, locate the lyrics online and project them for the participants to follow along. Invite the participants in these or similar words: "Let's reflectively — and prayerfully — listen to this song about the Holy Spirit before we close in prayer." Play the song for the gathering.

Session 5
The Good News

This session on the Good News explains the ageless importance of Scripture in the life of a Christian and how it relates to contemporary life. This presentation focuses not on the books of the Bible, but rather on how to understand and interpret its primary message of salvation history.

PREPARATION

Objectives	Handouts	Recommended Resources
To reflect upon the significance of Scripture by answering the question: Why is the word of God — Holy Scripture — essential in the life of a Christian? To ask and answer three related questions: What is the Good News? Is the Bible true? And is the Bible relevant today? To examine the importance of knowing the word of God.	Discussion questions "Today's Takeaway" slips (cut from the master sheet of three slips in the "Resource" section)	Bible Bookshelf

SESSION: THE GOOD NEWS

Greeting and Introduction (5 min.)

- ***Smile**, turn off the instrumental music, and call the session to order.*
- ***Thank*** the participants for coming back and for prioritizing their child's faith and sacramental formation. Say, "It's good to see everyone!"
- ***Ask*** them politely to silence their phones and refrain from looking at them during the session, barring a family emergency.
- ***Introduce** the session in these or similar words:*

This session's topic is the Good News. We'll answer some questions today, the central one being this: Why is the word of God essential to the lives of Christians?

We'll also answer three other questions:

- What is the "Good News"?
- Is the Bible true?
- Is the Bible relevant today?

First, let's review the topics we've covered in the four sessions we've had so far. We are halfway through this program!

Review (5 min.)

Remind the participants of the previous session, in these or similar words. Begin the PowerPoint presentation, if you are using it:

For the past four sessions, we've been establishing a platform upon which to examine, build, and shore up our faith in order to be able to help our children on their journey of faith.

Why? To become more aware of what is involved in being a strong, bold, and brave disciple of Jesus Christ.

Session 1 — Big Questions of Life: The answer to those questions is grounded in the bedrock of Jesus.

Session 2 — The God of Love and Mercy: God the Father is the first Person of the Trinity.

Session 3 — Who Do You Say That I Am? Jesus asked this question of his disciples and continues to ask everyone throughout the ages. He is the second Person of the Trinity.

Session 4 — The Comforter: The third Person of the Trinity — the Holy Spirit — comes to us as a comforter and friend, revealer of truth, intercessor, and indweller of believers.

What we learned from these sessions boils down to two things:

- What God is: A relationship of three persons.
- What God wants: A relationship with YOU!

Opening Prayer (2 min.)

- **Say,** "Let's open with a prayer."
- **Invite** those gathered to make the Sign of the Cross: "In the name of the Father, and of the Son, and of the Holy Spirit."
- **Read** the opening prayer as follows:

O Lord, our God, as we gather today to continue learning more about you, please open our hearts and minds to a greater understanding of how to seek and understand you through the Scriptures.

Please place in us the desire to seek you, to understand you, and in understanding you, to love you ever more.

We pray this in the name above all names — Jesus. Amen.

- **Conclude** the prayer with the Sign of the Cross.

Presentation (22 min.)

Begin the presentation in these or similar words:

The title of today's session is the Good News. Our key question is this: Why is the word of God essential in the life of a Christian?

Saint Paul wrote an epistle — another word for a letter — to Timothy, who was Paul's coworker along with Silas. His letter to Timothy explains the very basic purpose of Scripture: "All scripture is inspired by God and is useful for teaching, for reproof, for correction, and for training in righteousness, so that everyone who belongs to God may be proficient, equipped for every good work" (2 Tm 3:16–17).

According to the Cambridge English Dictionary, the word *reproof* means something that you say or do to show that you disapprove of someone's bad or silly behavior.

In this session, we aren't delving into specific parts of the Bible. Rather, we'll be answering four questions that most (if not all) of you probably have:

1. What is the "Good News"?

2. Is the Bible true?
3. Is the Bible relevant today?
4. Why is the word of God — Holy Scripture — essential in the life of a Christian?

1. What Is the "Good News"?

Present the origin of the word gospel in these or similar words:

The word *gospel* comes from Greek *euangelion* (pronounced "u-an-jell-ee-un"), which literally means "good news" or "good tidings." In ancient Greece *euangelion* denoted an important, authoritative, royal, or official message — usually to do with a military victory. Messengers who delivered or proclaimed the good news usually received a reward for doing so. Those who were the bearers of bad news were often punished at best or killed at worst.

The four Gospels — Matthew, Mark, Luke, and John — are written testaments to why Jesus is the Good News.

Explain what the Good News is, in these or similar words:

The Good News is that the saving acts of God — the cross and the Resurrection — were a redemption that healed the ruptured relationship between people and God due to original sin. Together they offered all of us the *hope* of salvation.

Our reward for hearing and living the redemption of the Good News is the *hope* of salvation, which is not to be confused with redemption.

Through the gift of God's grace, redemption refers to the act of Jesus sacrificially dying on the cross, so that we might be liberated from a life of slavery to sin to the freedom of a new life in and with him.

This act redeemed ALL of humanity.

Continue by explaining redemption as part of the history and process of our salvation:

Redemption is freely given to all — no asking necessary. It is Christ's invitation to salvation and is the first step in that process.

The process of salvation is as follows:

- Redemption
- Repentance
- Baptism
- Loving God
- Loving your neighbor
- Living a Christ-like life

Because God created us with free will, we choose how to respond to Christ's invitation.

Much is at stake if we decline Christ's invitation, so understanding salvation is critical. We can understand salvation in three ways:

- It is eternal life with God.
- It is a lifelong process that is our choice.
- It is ongoing, not a one-time event. A response is required when we receive the gift of redemption. The response is a lifelong decision to constantly choose Christ and follow the teachings of his Church.

Because salvation is not a one-time event, we can understand salvation to be a past, present, and future process. Being saved begins at baptism when the Holy Spirit comes to dwell in us, giving us the *capacity* to live a Christian life each day with the hope of eternal life with God in the future.

It is up to each person to either accept or reject God's gifts of redemption and the *hope* of salvation.

Return the discussion to the teachings of Saint Paul:

Saint Paul wrote to the Philippians: "Therefore, my beloved, just as you have always obeyed me, not only in my presence, but much more now in my absence, work out your own salvation with fear and trembling" (Phil 2:12).

The "work" that Saint Paul wrote about refers to our response to the will of God.

As Fr. Mike Schmitz says: "Salvation is being saved from being 'un-Christlike.'"[1]

2. Is the Bible True?

Introduce this second question about the Bible. Answer in these or similar words:

The Bible is true in the greater sense of truth, as the Church teaches: "Therefore, since everything asserted by the inspired authors or sacred writers must be held to be asserted by the Holy Spirit, it follows that the books of Scripture must be acknowledged as teaching solidly, faithfully and without error that truth which God wanted put into sacred writings for the sake of salvation."[2]

Inspired by the Holy Spirit, the Bible — both the Old and New Testaments — is the story of salvation history and the human drama that is touched and changed by God's grace.

The Good News of salvation was foretold throughout the Old Testament, beginning in Genesis with the story of Adam and Eve.

It culminates in the stories of Jesus and his disci-

ples found in the New Testament.

The Bible is God's way of communicating through human writers — inspired by the Holy Spirit — the stories of his presence, his love for us, and the experiences of Jesus recorded by witnesses to his life.

3. Is the Bible Relevant Today?

Introduce this third question about the Bible. Answer in these or similar words:

Today, many believe in or admire Jesus and what he stood for, but they don't really understand the Bible.

Some believe that the Bible — because it was written so long ago — has no real relevance to current societal and political problems and doesn't need to be taken that seriously.

However, to answer the question, *Is the Bible relevant today?* — the short answer is YES!

- The Bible is powerful.
- It is the best-selling book of all time.
- The gospel message — the Good News of Jesus — never grows old.
- It's the story of how God pursues us, loving and drawing us into a relationship because he desires our salvation.

When you understand the timelessness and relevance of the story and the message of the Bible as the inspired word of God, then you can understand just how important — indeed essential — it is in the life of a Christian.

4. Why Is Scripture Essential in the Christian Life?

Introduce this final question about the Bible. Answer in these or similar words:

Scripture is important in Christian life because it is a way for us to come to know Jesus better and his will for our life.

Scripture unites us with other Catholics. Worldwide, the same Scriptures are read at Mass each day.

The *Catechism* explains a truthful understanding of Scripture as inspired by the Holy Spirit: "God speaks to man in a human way" (109).

To better understand what God is saying through Scripture, we need to consider three things:

- Context — both historical and societal
- Tradition — the tradition of the whole Church, sometimes called Apostolic Tradition
- Teaching — the intimate relationship between Scripture and Tradition (the teaching of the Church), which are never in opposition to each other

Emphasize the point about the Church's Tradition, in these or similar words:

The second item, Church Tradition, is especially important. It comes from Christ and is the gift given to the apostles to be handed down to each generation.

Tradition stands alongside Scripture to form the teaching of the Church. Not everything Christ taught is contained in Scripture. The Gospel of John attests to this: "But there are also many other things that Jesus did; if every one of them were written down, I suppose that the world itself could not contain the books that would be written" (21:25).

Small-Group Discussion (20 min.)

Invite the groups to transition to small-group discussion time. Remind them to review the small-group discussion guidelines on the table tent, as needed.

Pass out the discussion questions handout. Explain the activity in these or similar words:

Please review the discussion questions handout.

Together discuss the questions on the handout you've been given. Answer as many as time allows.

Call everyone's attention back to you after twenty minutes.

Today's Takeaway (1 min.)

Direct the participants' attention to the slips of paper on their tables.

Give the following instructions:

- Please take a minute to write down something that struck you and that you'd like to reflect on or discuss with a friend, a spouse, or another participant.
- Please take this slip home and use it to prompt further reflection or discussion.

Closing (10 min.)

***Smile** and thank everyone for being there and participating. Tell them about the next session in these or similar words:*

Last week, we talked about the Holy Spirit, our Comforter. This week we talked about the Good News and why the word of God is essential in the life of a Christian.

Next week, we'll talk about faith and community.

Make any pertinent announcements. Point out where participants can obtain take-home resources on their way out.

Ask anyone who came in late to be sure to sign in before they leave, especially if you are keeping attendance.

- **Say**, "Let's close with a prayer."
- **Invite** those gathered to make the Sign of the Cross: "In the name of the Father, and of the Son, and of the Holy Spirit."
- **Read** the closing prayer as follows:

  May the Lord bless you and keep you. May the Lord make his face to shine upon you, and be gracious to you. And may the Lord grant you and yours peace. Amen. (based on Numbers 6:24–26, RSVCE)

- **Conclude** the prayer with the Sign of the Cross. Wish everyone a GREAT week!

Optional closing: Locate an MP3 or internet link for the song "Thy Word" (based on Ps 119:105), by Amy Grant. Try to locate a video of the song that displays the lyrics as they're sung. If you play an MP3 instead, locate the lyrics online and project them for the participants to follow along. Invite the participants in these or similar words: "Let's reflectively — and prayerfully — listen to this song about the word of God before we close in prayer." Play the song for the gathering.

Session 6

Faith and Community

This sixth session underscores the common theme of the entire program: namely, relationship. The presentation focuses on the importance of being involved in a faith community as a disciple of Jesus. Additionally, it explains why Mass attendance is important and necessary.

PREPARATION

Objectives

To explore the reasons for the importance of belonging to a faith community by asking and addressing four questions: Why do we need the Church — need to be part of a faith community? Why do we need to attend Mass? Is it possible to follow Jesus without religion — without the Church? And why is it important to have friends-in-Christ?

Handouts

Discussion questions

"Today's Takeaway" slips (cut from the master sheet of three slips in the "Resource" section)

Recommended Resources

"Why Do We 'Have To' Go to Mass?" pamphlet (OSV)

SESSION: FAITH AND COMMUNITY

Greeting and Introduction (5 min.)

- ***Smile**, turn off the instrumental music, and call the session to order.*
- ***Thank** the participants for coming back and for prioritizing their child's faith and sacramental formation. Say, "It's good to see everyone!"*
- ***Ask** them politely to silence their phones and refrain from looking at them during the session, barring a family emergency.*
- ***Introduce** the session in these or similar words:*

Last week's topic was the Good News. We answered one key question: Why is the word of God essential to the lives of Christians? We also answered three related questions: What is the "Good News"? Is the Bible true? And is the Bible relevant today?

This session's topic is faith and community. We'll examine four questions today:

- Why do we need the Church — need to be part of a faith community?
- Is it possible to follow Jesus without religion — without the Church?
- Why do we need to attend Mass?
- Why is it important to have friends-in-Christ?

First, let's review some things we covered in the previous session.

Review (5–7 min.)

Remind the participants of the previous session, in these or similar words. Begin the PowerPoint presentation, if you are using it:

Last week, we talked about the Good News and the importance of Scripture. We asked and answered four questions:

1. **What is the "Good News"?**
The word *gospel* comes from the Greek *euangelion*, which literally means "good news" or "good tidings."

The four Gospels — Matthew, Mark, Luke, and John — are written testaments as to why Jesus is the "Good News."

The "Good News" is that the saving acts of God — the cross and the Resurrection — were a redemption that healed the ruptured relationship between people and God — due to original sin — offering *all* the *hope* of salvation.

2. **Is the Bible true?**
The Bible is true in the greater sense of truth.

Inspired by the Holy Spirit, it is the story of salvation history and the human drama that is touched and changed by God's grace.

The Good News of salvation was foretold throughout the Old Testament and culminated in the stories of Jesus and his disciples in the New Testament.

The Bible is God's way of communicating through human writers — inspired by the Holy Spirit — the stories of his presence, his love for us, and the experiences of Jesus recorded by witnesses to his life.

3. **Is the Bible relevant today?**
The short answer: YES! The Bible is powerful. It is the bestselling book of all time.

The gospel message — the Good News of Jesus — never grows old.

It's the story of how God pursues us, loving and drawing us into a relationship because he desires our salvation.

4. **Given all that, why is Scripture essential in the Christian life?**
Through Scripture, we come to know Jesus better and his will for our life.

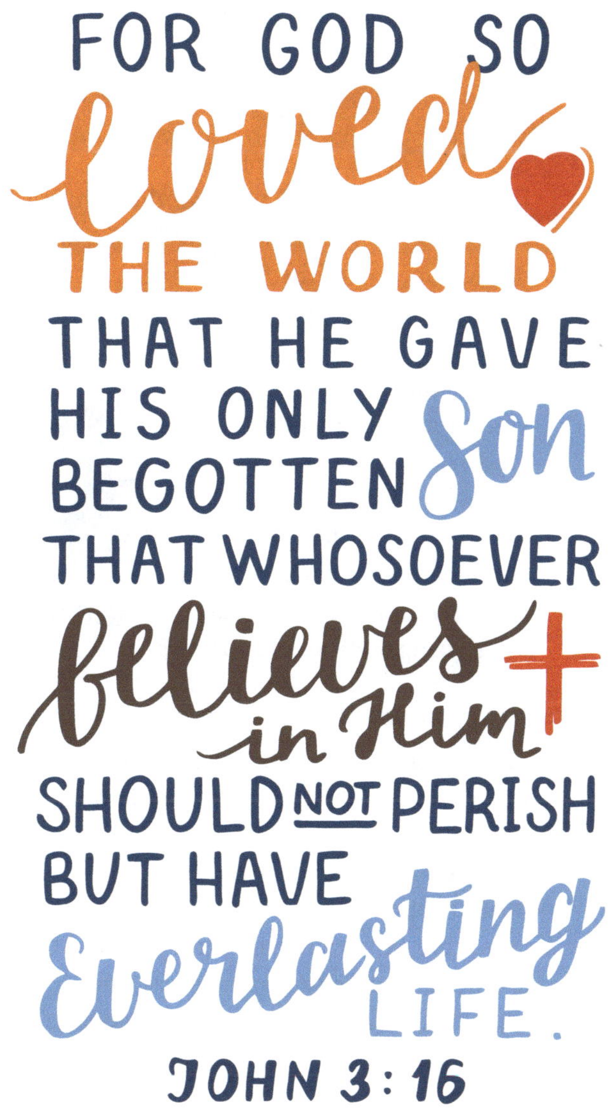

Scripture unites us with other Catholics. Worldwide, the same Scriptures are read at Mass each day.

The *Catechism* explains that a truthful understanding of Scripture is inspired by the Holy Spirit: "God speaks to man in a human way" (109).

Everything that we've talked about in the previous five sessions has been revealed throughout the ages in Sacred Scripture.

Ultimately, the Bible is about God's desire to be in relationship with us and about the extraordinary lengths he will go to in order to invite us into relationship. This desire is summed up in John 3:16: "For God so loved the world that he gave his only Son, so that everyone who believes in him may not perish but may have eternal life."

Point out that the common theme throughout every session thus far is relationship.

Opening Prayer (2 min.)

- **Say**, "Let's open with a prayer."
- **Invite** those gathered to make the Sign of the Cross: "In the name of the Father, and of the Son, and of the Holy Spirit."
- **Read** the opening prayer as follows:

> Dear God our Father: Thank you for all of your many gifts, blessings, and mercies that are bestowed on each of us daily.
>
> Thank you for the people you give us — our family and friends who journey with us in life, sharing our joys and sorrows — helping us in times of need.
>
> Thank you, especially, for the gift of your Son, Jesus, who — like us — knew and enjoyed the comfort of family and friends.
>
> We pray today that the Holy Spirit will enlighten our hearts and minds about the importance of belonging to a faith community. And we ask this in the name above all names — Jesus Christ, our Lord. Amen.

- **Conclude** with the Sign of the Cross.

Presentation (20 min.)

Begin the presentation in these or similar words.

This week we're talking about relationship again, and the importance of faith and community.

When we talked about Jesus in session 3, we talked about the importance of seeking an encounter with him and developing an ongoing relationship with him.

The Church teaches that the Scriptures were given to us in order that we might grow in right relationship with ourselves, our God, and one another. It's all about relationship!

Our encounter with Jesus results in a whole new life. That new life — as evidenced in the Acts of the Apostles — is to be nourished by the Church, which is the intersection between Christ and his believers.

Today we'll ask and answer four questions:

- Why do we need the Church — need to be part of a faith community?
- Why do we need to attend Mass?
- Is it possible to follow Jesus without religion — without the Church?
- Why is it important to have friends-in-Christ?

1. Why Do We Need the Church?

Introduce this first question about the Church. Answer in these or similar words:

Let's answer the first question, using an explanation provided by Bishop Don Hying of the Diocese of Madison, Wisconsin.[1]

Bishop Hying says that the Church, worldwide and parochially, is a community of people sharing faith together. You can't — and really don't — make the faith journey alone: You need the Church community, and the Church community needs you. Why do we need each other? For witness, prayer, and concern. We don't make it to heaven alone — a faith community encourages members along the way.

Explain that there are other reasons we need the Church:

The Church is the place of profound union with Christ and other believers.

The Church is the Body of Christ himself, and we are incorporated into that Body through baptism.

The Church provides the sacraments that are the channels connecting us to Jesus, the Source of Life, in a profound and visible way.

According to Scripture, the sacraments are rooted in Jesus' commands and examples.

The sacraments use natural elements — like water, bread, and oil — to communicate and give us Jesus' supernatural power and grace.

2. Why Do We Need to Attend Mass?

Introduce this second question about the Church. Answer in these or similar words:

Going to Mass fulfills the Third Commandment to keep holy the Lord's Day (see Ex 20:8). God asks us to set aside and make time for one holy day — "for it is written, "You shall be holy, for I am holy" (1 Pt 1:16).

Only at Mass can we experience the supernatural miracle of the common elements of bread and wine being changed into the Body and Blood of Christ. Each time we receive Jesus in the Eucharist, he is literally within us — he is as close to us as possible. The Eucharist is spiritual food like no other that gives us the grace and strength to follow Christ, nourishing us on our journey to eternal life in and with him.

According to Church teaching: "The Sunday Eucharist is the foundation and confirmation of all Christian practice. For this reason, the faithful are obliged to participate in the Eucharist on days of obligation, unless excused for a serious reason (for example, illness, the care of infants) or dispensed by their own pastor. Those who deliberately fail in this obligation commit a grave sin" (CCC 2181).

To deliberately miss Mass denies God's love and gift. Prioritizing another activity over Mass attendance is a form of idolatry, or worshiping of something else instead of God. So missing Mass breaks two commandments:

- First Commandment: I am the LORD your God; you shall not have strange Gods before me.
- Third Commandment: Keep holy the LORD's Day.

Only at Mass can you receive a special blessing and be commissioned to "go in peace, glorifying the Lord by your life," making the world a better place.

3. Is It Possible to Follow Jesus Without Religion — Without the Church?

Introduce this third question about the Church. Answer in these or similar words:

The short answer is NO! We simply cannot follow Jesus without the Church.

But why?

Many believe in and know about Jesus. That's not enough. We also need to follow Jesus. To follow Jesus, we need to be part of a church community.

Point out the role of community in Jesus' mission:

Community was central to Jesus' mission, and it remains a core teaching of his Church.

For example, Jesus' miracles of healing people had a larger significance than just curing them. During Jesus' time, if you were afflicted with leprosy or blindness, or you were mired in serious sin (like the woman at the well), you were an outcast.

When Jesus encountered a person in need of healing and healed them, that person was transformed and was restored to the fullness of their community.

Other biblical evidence of the importance of community in Jesus' teachings is how he taught his disciples to pray. He did not instruct them to say, "*My father*" but, rather "*Our Father.*" The Lord's Prayer says, "give *us* this day *our* daily bread" (see Mt 6:9–13, emphases added).

4. Why Is It Important to Have Friends-in-Christ?

Introduce this final question about the Church. Answer in these or similar words:

Pope Francis says that the Church is a "field hospital for sinners."[2] What does that mean?

The presence of others in our lives compels us to break out of our self-centered daily routines and to ask how we might serve others: how we might feed the hungry, provide shelter to the homeless, and care for the sick, orphaned, bereaved, and heartbroken.

Friends in Christ model for us discipleship in the community of faith, and they challenge us to do the same.

Too often we hear about folks who say, "I pray, but I don't see the need to show up to church or be part of organized religion." Or "I'm spiritual but not religious." In response, point out that people thrive both spiritually and psychologically within a community of people that will encourage, sustain, and support them.

Conclude by further explaining how our spiritual life benefits from community.

The community of faith we call "church" helps us survive a broken heart, forces us to confront the ethical and moral implications of our lifestyle, and helps us navigate difficult decisions.

We cannot live out our commitment to Jesus as disciples without the community of the Church and friends-in-Christ, because people need love, support, fellowship, and accountability.

The Church provides us a place where we can build relationships with other Christians.

Small-Group Discussion (20 min.)

Invite the groups to transition to small-group discussion time. Remind them to review the small-group discussion guidelines on the table tent, as needed.

Pass out the discussion questions handout. Explain the activity in these or similar words:

Please review the discussion questions handout.

Together discuss the questions on the handout you've been given. Answer as many as time allows.

Call everyone's attention back to you after twenty minutes.

Today's Takeaway (1 min.)

Direct the participants' attention to the slips of paper on their tables.

Give the following instructions:

- Please take a minute to write down something that struck you and that you'd like to reflect on or discuss with a friend, a spouse, or another participant.
- Please take this slip home and use it to prompt further reflection or discussion.

Closing (10 min.)

***Smile** and thank everyone for being there and participating. Tell them about the next session in these or similar words:*

Last week, we talked about the Good News and why the word of God is essential in the life of a Christian. This week we talked about faith and community.

Next week, we'll talk about the power of prayer.

Make any pertinent announcements. Point out where participants can obtain take-home resources on their way out.

Ask anyone who came in late to be sure to sign in before they leave, especially if you are keeping attendance.

- **Say**, "Let's close with a prayer."
- **Invite** those gathered to make the Sign of the Cross: "In the name of the Father and of the Son and of the Holy Spirit."
- **Read** the closing prayer as follows:

  May the Lord bless you and keep you. May the Lord make his face to shine upon you, and be gracious to you. And may the Lord grant you and yours peace. Amen. (Based on Nm 6:24–26, RSVCE)

- **Conclude** the prayer with the Sign of the Cross. Wish everyone a GREAT week!

Optional closing: Locate an MP3 or internet link for the song "The Servant Song," by Richard Gillard. Try to locate a video of the song that displays the lyrics as they're sung. If you play an MP3 instead, locate the lyrics online and project them for the participants to follow along. Invite the participants in these or similar words: "Let's reflectively — and prayerfully — listen to this song about what it means to be part of the Church, before we close in prayer." Play the song for the gathering.

Session 7

The Power of Prayer

This seventh session explains just how powerful and unlimiting prayer is in its various forms. This presentation focuses on the rationale behind prayer, rather than on specific prayers or those prayers unique to Catholicism.

PREPARATION

Objectives

To examine the importance of prayer by asking and answering two questions: What is prayer? And why should we pray?

To explain the value of prayer in participants' lives and the lives of their families.

Handouts

Discussion questions

"Today's Takeaway" slips (cut from the master sheet of three slips in the "Resource" section)

Recommended Resources

Basic Catholic prayers handout

SESSION: THE POWER OF PRAYER

Greeting and Introduction (5 min.)

- ***Smile****, turn off the instrumental music, and call the session to order.*
- ***Thank*** the participants for coming back and for prioritizing their child's faith and sacramental formation. Say, "It's good to see everyone!"
- ***Ask*** them politely to silence their phones and refrain from looking at them during the session, barring a family emergency.
- ***Introduce*** *the session in these or similar words:*

Last week, we talked about faith and community. We answered four questions: Why do we need the Church — to be part of a faith community? Why do we need to attend Mass? Is it possible to follow Jesus without religion, without the Church? And why is it important to have friends-in-Christ?

This session's topic is the power of prayer. We'll ask and answer two questions:

- What is prayer?
- Why should we pray?

This is the seventh session of eight. For the last six sessions we've been covering topics that will, hopefully, bring you to a greater awareness of your important role as you accompany your child on their own journey of faith as disciples of Jesus Christ.

This session on prayer focuses on the rationale behind prayer, rather than specific prayers or prayers that are unique to Catholicism.

First, let's review some things we covered in the previous session.

Review (5–7 min.)

Remind the participants of the previous session, in these or similar words. Begin the PowerPoint presentation, if you are using it:

When we talked about faith and community, we asked and answered four questions:

1. Why do we need the Church — need to be part of a faith community?

You need the Church community — and the Church community needs you — for witness, prayer, and concern.

We don't make it to heaven alone. A faith community encourages us along the way.

The Church is the place of profound union with Christ and other believers.

The Church provides the sacraments that are the channels that connect us to Jesus, the Source of Life, in a profound and visible way.

2. Why do we need to attend Mass?

It's one of the Ten Commandments.

Only at Mass can we experience the supernatural miracle in which the common elements of bread and wine are changed into the Body and Blood of Christ in the Eucharist.

Purposefully missing or avoiding Mass — except for illness or another serious emergency — is, frankly, a sin. Prioritizing another activity over Mass attendance is a form of idolatry.

3. Is it possible to follow Jesus without religion — without the Church?

The short answer is — no! But why?

Many believe in and know about Jesus. We also need to follow. If you follow Jesus, then you will become part of a church community. Community was central to Jesus' mission, and it remains a core teaching of his Church. Jesus' miracles of healing people had a larger significance than just curing them. Those whom he healed were transformed and restored to the fullness of their community. When he taught his disciples to pray, he instructed them to say not "My father" but "Our Father" and "give *us* this day *our* daily bread" (Mt 6:9–13).

4. Why is it important to have friends-in-Christ?

Pope Francis says that the Church is a "field hospital for sinners."

Friends-in-Christ model discipleship in the community of faith, and they challenge us to do the same.

The Church provides us a place to build relationships with other Christians who will sustain and support us.

The Church's community of faith helps us navigate the joys and the challenges of life.

We cannot live out a total commitment to Jesus as disciples without the community of the Church and friends-in-Christ.

Opening Prayer (2 min.)

- **Say**, "Let's open with a prayer."
- **Invite** those gathered to make the Sign of the Cross: "In the name of the Father, and of the Son, and of the Holy Spirit."
- **Read** the opening prayer as follows:

Dear Heavenly Father,

Thank you for this day and for the promise that you will give us whatever we ask of you in the name of Jesus if it is in your will to do so.

We pray that you will open our hearts and minds in order that we might love you and others more dearly. Help us to hear your voice calling in the night and to recognize and appreciate your mighty works among your creation. Help us to grow in faith and increase our gratitude for the gifts of your presence and your Word.

We pray this through Christ, our Lord. Amen.

- **Conclude** the prayer with the Sign of the Cross.

Presentation (20 min.)

Begin the presentation in these or similar words.

The topic of this session is prayer.

We'll explore the power of prayer by asking and answering two questions:

1. What is prayer?
2. Why should we pray?

1. What Is Prayer?

Introduce this first question about prayer. Answer in these or similar words:

The answer to the first question is rather simple: To quote Bishop Donald Hying of Madison, Wisconsin, "Prayer is nurturing our relationship with God."[1]

We can think of prayer in two other ways:

- It is a gift of God's grace.
- It is the work of the Holy Spirit that draws us closer into a relationship with God.

Mark Hart says that "prayer doesn't 'help' our relationship with God, prayer IS our relationship with God."[2]

Explain that there are two categories of prayer: public and private (or personal). Present each category in these or similar words:

Public prayer is the easiest form of prayer, and the easiest form to identify. Sometimes it is scripted and led by a priest, deacon, or lay minister.

Private prayer is another matter and one that many struggle with. People often say, "I just don't know how to pray." However, private prayer has several options:

- **Vocal:** Mental or audible words through which we communicate our feelings, wants, and needs (see CCC 2700). These include memorized prayers like the Our Father and Hail Mary.
- **Meditation:** A quest to find out what the Lord wants from us and to strengthen our will to follow Christ by engaging thought, imagination, emotion, and desire (CCC 2705).
- **Contemplative:** Silence as you spend time with Christ, becoming one with him (CCC 2709).

Acknowledge that we all face obstacles to private prayer from time to time:

Even with these options, we often encounter obstacles to private prayer:

- Time
- Distractions
- Forgetfulness
- Feeling dry or distant from God
- Insecurity or feelings of unworthiness
- Fear of God's will

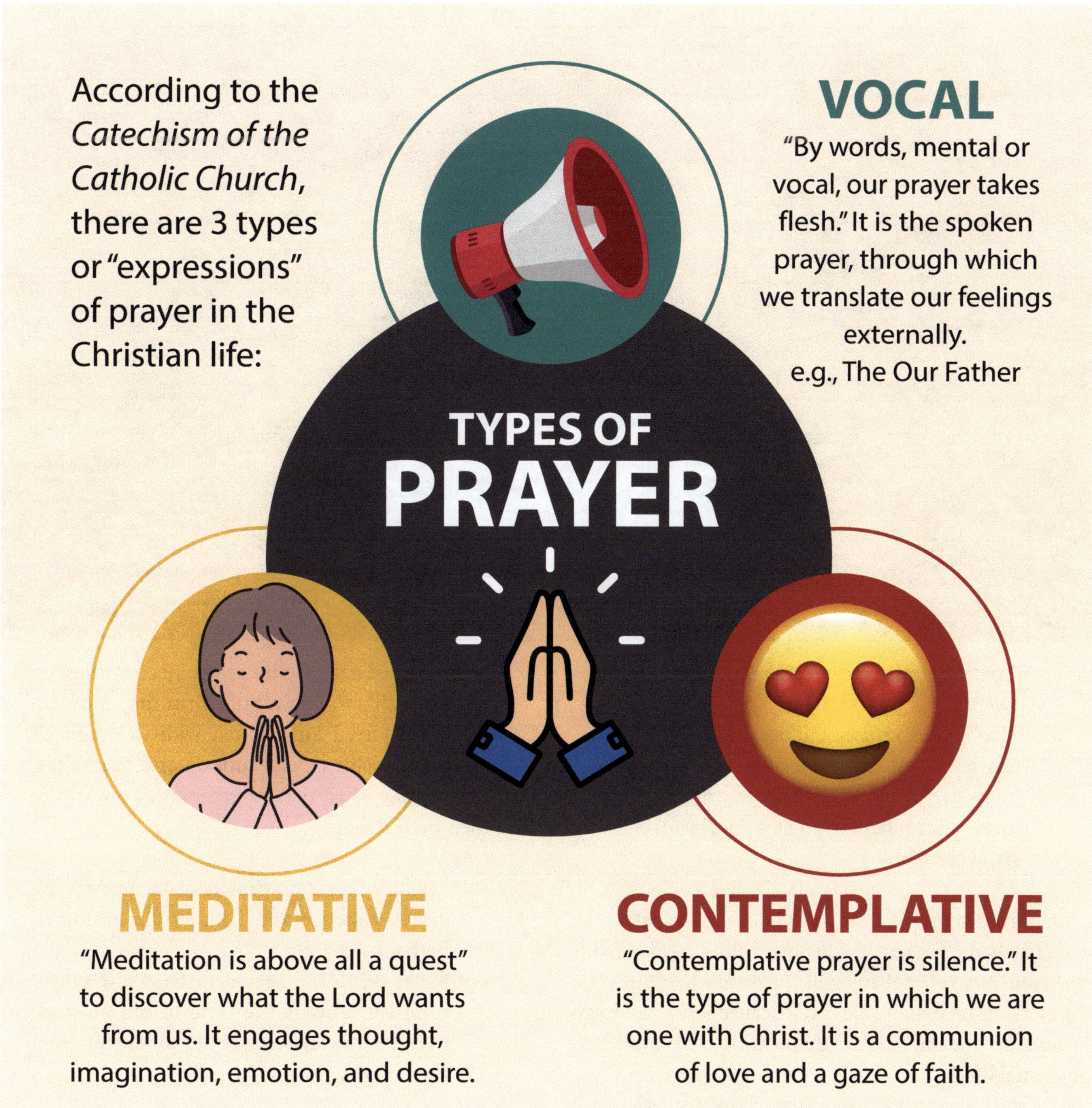

"Thy will be done" can be the most frightening prayer of all — but it's how Jesus told us to pray: first when he taught us the Lord's Prayer, and most profoundly when he prayed it himself in the garden at Gethsemane.

2. Why Should We Pray?

Introduce this second question about prayer, and acknowledge that we all ask it sometimes. Answer in these or similar words:

We pray because prayer gives us the opportunity to communicate with God and gives the Holy Spirit the opportunity to work for and within us.

But when we pray, WE WANT ANSWERS! However, God isn't a vending machine, and if we're only praying when we want something, we're approaching prayer the wrong way. What answers can we expect when we pray?

- **"Yes":** We ask and receive the desired answer.
- **"No":** God refuses our request, either for our good, for the good of others, or both. Consider these scriptural examples, and know that when you get a "no," you're in good company.

Jesus prayed in the garden of Gethsemane before he was crucified, "Father, if you are willing, remove this cup from me; yet, not my will but yours be done" (Lk 22:42). God the Father said "no" because Jesus had to go through his passion in order that we might have the *hope* for eternal life.

Saint Paul prayed that a "thorn" be removed in 2 Corinthians 12:7–10:

> Even considering the exceptional character of the revelations. Therefore, to keep me from being too elated, a thorn was given me in the flesh, a messenger of Satan to torment me, to keep me from being too elated. Three times I appealed to the Lord about this, that it would leave me, but he said to me, "My grace is sufficient for you, for power is made perfect in weakness." So, I will boast all the more gladly of my weaknesses, so that the power of Christ may dwell in me. Therefore, I am content with weaknesses, insults, hardships, persecutions, and calamities for the sake of Christ; for whenever I am weak, then I am strong.

- **"Wait":** Not a no or a yes, this answer requires patience and faith as the timing is perhaps not right.
- **"Silence":** God seems distant and unresponsive. This is the time to draw closer to Jesus in prayer for better understanding and insight.

Conclude by emphasizing that God always hears and answers our prayers in his own way:

In the movie *Let There Be Light*, Katy Harkens (played by Sam Sorbo) says, "God always answers prayers, sometimes we just don't understand the answers."[3]

Keep this in mind as we transition to small-group discussion.

Small-Group Discussion (20 min.)

Invite the groups to transition to small-group discussion time. Remind them to review the small-group discussion guidelines on the table tent, as needed.

Pass out the discussion questions handout. Explain the activity in these or similar words:

Please review the discussion questions handout.

Together discuss the questions on the handout you've been given. Answer as many as time allows.

Call everyone's attention back to you after twenty minutes.

Today's Takeaway (1 min.)

Direct the participants' attention to the slips of paper on their tables.

Give the following instructions:

- Please take a minute to write down something that struck you and that you'd like to reflect on or discuss with a friend, a spouse, or another participant.
- Please take this slip home and use it to prompt further reflection or discussion.

Closing (10 min.)

***Smile** and thank everyone for being there and participating. Tell them about the next session in these or similar words:*

Last week, we talked about faith and community. This week we talked about the power of prayer.

Next week, we'll talk about "listening to that still, small voice."

Make any pertinent announcements. Point out where participants can obtain take-home resources on their way out.

Ask anyone who came in late to be sure to sign in before they leave, especially if you are keeping attendance.

- **Say**, "Let's close with a prayer."
- **Invite** those gathered to make the Sign of the Cross: "In the name of the Father, and of the Son, and of the Holy Spirit."
- **Read** the closing prayer as follows:

  May the Lord bless you and keep you.
  May the Lord make his face to shine upon you, and be gracious to you.
  And may the Lord grant you and yours peace. Amen. (Based on Nm 6:24–26, RSVCE)

- **Conclude** the prayer with the Sign of the Cross. Wish everyone a GREAT week!

Optional closing: Locate an MP3 or internet link for the song "Thy Will," by Hillary Scott and The Scott Family. Try to locate a video of the song that displays the lyrics as they're sung. If you play an MP3 instead, locate the lyrics online and project them for the participants to follow along. Invite the participants in these or similar words: "Let's reflectively — and prayerfully — listen to this song about prayer, before we close in our own prayer." Play the song for the gathering.

Session 8

Listening to That Still, Small Voice

This eighth and final session completes the presentation on the topic of prayer and concludes the program.

PREPARATION

Objectives

To discover how to discern God's will for our lives through prayer by asking and answering the question, Does God speak to us?

To explore how God speaks to people in prayer, and that his voice will guide them and their families on the right path.

Handouts

Discussion questions

"Today's Takeaway" slips (cut from the master sheet of three slips in the "Resource" section)

Recommended Resources

"*Amoris Laetitia*: On Love in the Family" pamphlet (OSV)

"10 Things that Make for a Great Catholic Family" pamphlet (OSV)

"10 Things that Make for a Great Catholic Mom" pamphlet (OSV)

"10 Things that Make for a Great Catholic Dad" pamphlet (OSV)

SESSION: LISTENING TO THAT STILL, SMALL VOICE

Greeting and Introduction (5 min.)

- ***Smile***, *turn off the instrumental music, and call the session to order.*
- ***Thank*** the participants for coming back and for prioritizing their child's faith and sacramental formation. Say, "It's good to see everyone!"
- ***Ask*** them politely to silence their phones and refrain from looking at them during the session, barring a family emergency.
- ***Introduce*** *the session in these or similar words:*

This is the eighth and final session of our time together.

For seven sessions we've covered topics that will bring you to a greater awareness of your important role as you accompany your child on their own journey of faith as disciples of Jesus Christ.

The final topic is listening to that "still, small voice." We'll ask and answer just one question today: Does God speak to us? This follow-up session on prayer focuses on whether and how God speaks to us.

First, let's review some things we covered in the previous session.

Review (5–7 min.)

Remind the participants of the previous session, in these or similar words. Begin the PowerPoint presentation, if you are using it:

We asked and answered two questions:

1. **What is prayer?**

The first question — What is prayer? — had a simple answer, borrowing from Bishop Donald Hying: "Prayer is nurturing our relationship with God."

Other answers include the following points:

- Prayer is a gift of God's grace.
- It is the work of the Holy Spirit that draws us closer into a relationship with God.

There are two categories of prayer: public and private.

Public prayer is the easiest — scripted, memorized, led by a priest, deacon or lay minister.

Private prayer, however, is one that many struggle with. People often say, "I just don't know how to pray."

In private prayer we have several options:

- Vocal
- Meditative
- Contemplative

Even with these options, there are often obstacles to private prayer:

- Time
- Distractions
- Forgetfulness
- Feeling dry or distant from God
- Insecurity or feelings of unworthiness
- Fear of God's will (In fact, "Thy will be done" can be the most frightening prayer of all — but it's how Jesus told us to pray.)

2. Why should we pray?

Prayer gives us the opportunity to communicate with God and gives the Holy Spirit the opportunity to work for and within us.

This is a valid response. But when we pray, we want answers! What answers can we expect when we pray?

Yes: We ask and receive the desired answer.

No: God refuses our request either for our good, for the good of others, or both. Jesus prayed in the garden of Gethsemane before he was crucified: "Father, if you are willing, remove this cup from me; yet, not my will but yours be done" (Lk 22:42). God the Father said no, because Jesus had to go through his passion so that we might have the hope for eternal life. And Saint Paul prayed that a "thorn" be removed in 2 Corinthians 12:7–10. So, when you get a "no," you're in good company.

Wait: Not a no, this answer requires patience and faith. It means the timing isn't right for a full yes.

Silence: God sometimes seems distant and unresponsive. This is the time to draw closer to Jesus in prayer for better understanding and insight.

And God always hears and answers our prayers, even if we don't understand the answer.

Opening Prayer (2 min.)

- **Say**, "Let's open with a prayer."
- **Invite** those gathered to make the Sign of the Cross: "In the name of the Father, and of the Son, and of the Holy Spirit."
- **Read** the opening prayer as follows:

Dear Heavenly Father,

Thank you for this day and for the promise that you will give us whatever we ask of you in the name of Jesus if it is in your will to do so.

We pray that you will open our hearts and minds in order that we might love you and others more dearly, confident that you are near, waiting patiently and lovingly for us to turn to you. Help us to hear your voice calling in the night and to recognize and appreciate your mighty works among your creation. Increase our faith and gratitude for the gifts of your presence and your Word.

We pray this through Christ, our Lord. Amen.

- **Conclude** the prayer with the Sign of the Cross.

Presentation (20 min.)

Begin the presentation in these or similar words:

The topic of our final session is related to our previous session on prayer: specifically, let's examine how we hear God's voice:

- In public prayer — especially in the ultimate prayer, the Mass
- In private prayer — through verbal, meditative, or contemplative prayer

Let's look at these two categories more closely:

Public prayer: The Mass is the greatest prayer of the Church. This is because the Eucharist is the single greatest source of grace wherein Jesus gives his Body and Blood as food for our spiritual life. The Eucharist gives us the strength to, as the priest or deacon states in the Concluding Rites: "Go in peace, glorifying the Lord by your life."

Private prayer: Praying privately is how we discern, especially when we face the tough decisions. However, we have to be careful when discerning. According to Saint Ignatius of Loyola, we aren't neutral territory. Each of us is a battleground between the Spirit of God and the spirits who follow the evil one, who often come to us posing as beautiful angels of light. Ultimately, correct discernment cannot be at odds with either Scripture or Tradition.

Continue to this session's question and answer in these or similar words:

Let's answer the one question we're asking this session: Does God speak to us? People often wonder about someone who claims to hear God speak to them. The reality is that, yes, God does speak to us — but how?

- God speaks to us through the power of the Holy Spirit. Heaven and earth meet.
- God speaks to us through whispers and mysteries.
- God doesn't overwhelm us.

Tell the participants that these concepts are illustrated in Elijah's encounter with God in the Old Testament:

After his victory over the prophets of the idol Baal, the prophet Elijah learned that the king of Israel's wife, Jezebel, wanted him killed, so he ran into the desert. God had to send an angel with food and water so that he would survive. God then instructed Elijah to go to Horeb, where the prophet hid in a cave.

While there, Elijah complained to God that every one of his prophets — except Elijah — had been killed by Jezebel's command. God instructed him to come out of the cave and stand on the mountain in his presence, as we read in the First Book of Kings:

> And he said, "Go forth, and stand upon the mount before the Lord." And behold, the Lord passed by, and a great and strong wind tore the mountains, and broke in pieces the rocks before the Lord, but the Lord was not in the wind; and after the wind an earthquake, but the Lord was not in the earthquake; and after the earthquake a fire, but the Lord was not in the fire; and after the fire a **still small voice.** (19:11–12, RSV2CE)

Finally, after all those dramatic events of wind and earthquake and fire, we read that God spoke to Elijah in a "still small voice." That account is the only place in Scripture where God is said to speak in a "still small voice."

The point of this story is to show that God works quietly, as the prophet Zechariah wrote: "Not by might, nor by power, but by my spirit" (Zec 4:6).

Pause and answer the question of the presentation: How can we cultivate our ability to discern — to hear that "still small voice" of God?

Answer the question in these or similar words:

We cultivate that ability in two ways:

- Through prayer
- Through studying God's Word — especially the New Testament

Small-Group Discussion (20 min.)

Invite the groups to transition to small-group discussion time. Remind them to review the small-group discussion guidelines on the table tent, as needed.

Pass out the discussion questions handout. Explain the activity in these or similar words:

Please review the discussion questions handout.

Together discuss the questions on the handout you've been given. Answer as many as time allows.

Call everyone's attention back to you after twenty minutes.

Today's Takeaway (1 min.)

Direct the participants' attention to the slips of paper on their tables.

Give the following instructions:

- Please take a minute to write down something that struck you and that you'd like to reflect on or discuss with a friend, a spouse, or another participant.
- Please take this slip home and use it to prompt further reflection or discussion.

Closing (10 min.)

Smile and thank everyone for being there and participating. Tell them what an honor and a blessing it has been to serve them — and by extension their families.

Make any pertinent announcements. Point out where participants can obtain take-home resources on their way out.

Optional Handouts: If you are able to give a Bible and/or a Mass book to each family, announce that you have one gift bag for each family, with the family's name on the bag. Invite one family member to pick up their bag on their way out. Alternatively, hand out the gifts bags so that two people from the same family don't inadvertently pick up two.

Ask anyone who came in late to be sure to sign in before they leave, especially if you are keeping attendance.

- **Say**, "Let's close with a prayer" after the song.
- **Invite** those gathered to make the Sign of the Cross: "In the name of the Father, and of the Son, and of the Holy Spirit."
- **Read** the closing prayer as follows:

  May the Lord bless you and keep you.
  May the Lord make his face to shine upon you, and be gracious to you.
  And may the Lord grant you and yours peace. Amen. (Based on Nm 6:24–26, RSVCE)

- **Conclude** the prayer with the Sign of the Cross. Wish everyone a GREAT week!

Optional closing 1: Locate an MP3 or internet link for the song "The Blessing" (radio version), by Kari Jobe. Try to locate a video of the song that displays the lyrics as they're sung. If you play an MP3 instead, locate the lyrics online and project them for the participants to follow along.

Invite the participants in these or similar words: "Let's reflectively — and prayerfully — listen to this song before we close in prayer." Play the song for the gathering.

Conclude by inviting those gathered to make a final Sign of the Cross — no other closing prayer is necessary, as the song itself is the prayer.

Optional closing 2: Locate an MP3 or internet link for the song "Word of God Speak," by MercyMe. Try to locate a video of the song that displays the lyrics as they're sung. If you play an MP3 instead, locate the lyrics online and project them for the participants to follow along.

Invite the participants in these or similar words: "Let's reflectively — and prayerfully — listen to this song before we close in prayer." Play the song for the gathering.

Recommendations for Next Steps

After the first time I conducted the program, I was pleasantly surprised when several participants asked for a continuation of some kind, as they wanted to learn more and continue seeing friends they had made. To me, their request was evidence that they had experienced primary evangelization and formed a community.

Situations like this provide opportunities for continuous formation in other group settings — like a Bible study. If you have another adult faith formation offering scheduled during the same time period, then recommend that the parents investigate joining. This will work if your parish uses an at-home preparation program that parents or guardians follow with their children outside of the classroom.

Other parishes use an integrated intergenerational family catechesis program for sacrament preparation. If this is true of your parish, then you can promote a natural, organic transition as parents join their children in their sacrament preparation classes.

One approach isn't necessarily better than the other. The guiding principle is to provide another program for participants to transition into so they can maintain interest, momentum, and engagement with the parish community.

Notes

Introduction

1. Christian Smith and Patricia Snell, *Souls in Transition: The Religious and Spiritual Lives of Emerging Adults* (New York: Oxford University Press, 2009), 280.

2. Pew Research Center, *America's Changing Religious Landscape: Christians Decline Sharply as Share of Population, Unaffiliated and Other Faiths Continue to Grow* (Washington, DC: Pew Research Center, May 12, 2015), 35–40.

3. Thomas P. Rausch, *Being Catholic in a Culture of Choice* (Collegeville, MN: Liturgical Press, 2006), 18.

4. Mark M. Gray, *The Catholic Family: 21st Century Challenges in the United States*; *The US Catholic Family: Demographics*; *Practice of Faith in the Catholic Family*; *Catholic Families and Media Usage* (Washington, DC: The Center for Applied Research in the Apostolate and Holy Cross Family Ministries, 2015), 1–13.

5. Vatican II, Dogmatic Constitution *Lumen Gentium* (The Church), par. 11, in *Vatican Council II: The Conciliar and Post-Conciliar Documents*, ed. Austin Flannery (Northport, NY: Costello Publishing Co., 1996), 1:362.

6. Michael Paul Gallagher, *Clashing Symbols: An Introduction to Faith and Culture* (New York: Paulist Press, 1998), 112.

7. Sherry A. Weddell, *Forming Intentional Disciples: The Path to Knowing and Following Jesus* (Huntington, IN: Our Sunday Visitor Publishing Division, 2012), 46.

8. Francis, Apostolic Exhortation *Evangelii Gaudium* (The Joy of the Gospel), par. 7 (Boston: Pauline Books and Media, 2013), 5.

9. John Paul II, Apostolic Exhortation *Catechesi Tradendae* (On Catechesis in Our Time), vatican.va, par. 19, emphasis added.

10. Ralph Martin, "The Post-Christendom Sacramental Crisis: The Wisdom of Thomas Aquinas," *Nova et Vetera* (English Edition) 11, no. 1 (Winter 2013): 68.

11. *Catechism of the Catholic Church,* 2nd ed. (Libreria Editrice Vaticana), 1131.

12. Weddell, *Forming Intentional Disciples*, 46.

13. Tom Quinlan, *Excellence in Ministry: Best Practices for Successful Catechetical Leadership* (Chicago: Loyola Press, 2017), 49–50.

14. Francis, General Audience, May 20, 2015, vatican.va.

15. Charles Taylor, *A Secular Age* (Cambridge, MA: The Belknap Press of Harvard University Press, 2007), 1–3.

16. Avery Cardinal Dulles, "John Paul II and the Advent of the New Millennium," in *Church and Society: The Laurence J. McGinley Lectures, 1988–2007* (New York: Fordham University Press, 2008), 195.

17. Pontifical Council for the Family, Symposium of the College of Cardinals, Intervention by Cardinal Alfonso Lopez Trujillo: "The Family in the Pontificate of John Paul II," 2003, Introduction, vatican.va.

18. Avery Cardinal Dulles, "The Impact of the Catholic Church on American Culture," in *Evangelizing America*, ed. Thomas P. Rausch, SJ (Mahwah, NJ: Paulist Press, 2004), 20.

19. Robert S. Rivers, "Evangelization in the Contemporary Church," in *Evangelizing America*, ed. Thomas P. Rausch SJ (Mahwah, NJ: Paulist Press, 2004), 59.

20. John Paul II, Encyclical Letter *Centesimus Annus* (Hundredth Year), vatican.va., par. 41.

21. Francis, *The Joy of the Gospel*, 120.

22. John Paul II, Homily at Mass at The Shrine of the Holy Cross, Mogila, vatican.va., par. 1.

23. Vatican II, Pastoral Constitution *Gaudium et Spes* (On the Church in the Modern World), December 7, 1965, in *Vatican Council II: The Conciliar and Post-Conciliar Documents*, ed. Austin Flannery (Northport, NY: Costello Publishing Co., 1996), no. 1.

24. The United States Conference of Catholic Bishops (USCCB), "New Evangelization," https://www.usccb.org/beliefs-and-teachings/how-we-teach/new-evangelization.

25. Benedict XVI, General Audience, September 3, 2008, vatican.va.

26. Ibid., October 21, 2009, vatican.va.

27. Ibid., September 3, 2008, vatican.va.

28. Pope Francis, Homily at Mass in Saint Francis Square, Assisi, October 4, 2013, vatican.va.

29. Christian Smith and Melinda Lundquist Denton, *Soul Searching: The Religious and Spiritual Lives of American Teenagers* (New York:

Oxford University Press, 2005), 4, 162–163.

30. Smith and Denton, 163.

31. Ibid., 163–164.

32. Ibid., 164–165.

33. Ibid., 171.

34. Michael Patrick Barber, *Salvation: What Every Catholic Should Know* (San Francisco: Ignatius Press, 2019), 81.

35. Mike Schmitz, *Are You Saved? The Catholic Understanding of Salvation* (West Chester, PA: Ascension, 2021), 4–6.

36. John Paul II, Apostolic Exhortation *Catechesi Tradendae* (On Catechesis in Our Time), vatican.va., par. 18–19.

37. Pope Francis, Homily at Casa Santa Marta, May 3, 2018, available at "Pope: Faith Is Transmitted through Witness and Love," *Asia News*, http://www.asianews.it/news-en/Pope:-faith-is-transmitted-through-witness-and-love-43782.html.

38. Tom Corcoran and Michael J. White, *Rebuilt: Awakening the Faithful, Reaching the Lost, Making Church Matter* (Notre Dame, IN: Ave Maria Press, 2013).

39. James Mallon, *Divine Renovation: From a Maintenance to a Mission Parish* (New London, CT: Twenty Third Publications, 2014).

SESSION 3
Who Do You Say That I Am?

1. Adapted from the prayer of St. Richard of Chichester, available at https://www.catholicdigest.com/from-the-magazine/quiet-moment/prayer-st-richard-chichester-thanks-thee/.

SESSION 4
The Comforter

1. C. S. Lewis, "The Shocking Alternative," *Mere Christianity* (New York: A Touchstone Book, 1996), 54–56.

SESSION 5
The Good News

1. Schmitz, 6.

2. Dogmatic Constitution *Dei Verbum* (The Word of God) in *Vatican Council II: The Conciliar and Post-Conciliar Documents*, ed. Austin Flannery (Northport, NY: Costello, 1996), par. 11.

SESSION 6
Faith and Community

1. Bishop Donald Hying, "C4: Ignite Your Catholic Faith: Why Do I Need Church?" Archdiocese of Milwaukee, November 24, 2012, https://www.youtube.com/watch?v=W3A5KXu5__w.

2. Antonio Spadaro, Interview with Pope Francis, vatican.va.

SESSION 7
The Power of Prayer

1. Bishop Donald Hying, "C4: Ignite Your Catholic Faith: What is Prayer?" Archdiocese of Milwaukee, September 27, 2013, https://www.youtube.com/watch?v=_qlS3ynVdcc.

2. Mark Hart, *A Second Look: Encountering the True Jesus* (Huntington, IN: Our Sunday Visitor, 2016).

3. *Let There Be Light* official trailer, October 1, 2017, video available at https://www.youtube.com/watch?v=xwRmua7YLTk&t=93s.

About the Author

Marylynn Wesson has served in Church ministry for more than twenty years. The depth and breadth of her experience includes serving in the following capacities: on a diocesan RCIA task force; as a parish director of discipleship formation; as a parish RCIA director; and as a pastoral associate with a ministry to the homebound, sick, elderly, and bereaved. She also has experience teaching theology and world religions at both the high school and college level, as well as business experience in the private sector.

Her undergraduate degree in the humanities is from Southern Methodist University, and her master's in theological studies is from the University of Dallas. Her theological studies have culminated in the attainment of a doctor of ministry degree from The Catholic University of America with a concentration in her ministerial passion and focus: evangelization.

Marylynn lives in the Archdiocese of Galveston-Houston in Richmond, Texas, with her husband, Dr. Gary Wesson. They both feel blessed to have three grown children and their spouses who are successfully "adulting," two "grandcats," two "granddogs," and two absolutely yummy grandsons.

Resources and Handouts

This section includes the discussion questions and handouts for each session. You can photocopy these resources straight from this book, or you can access printable downloads of the handouts at firmfoundation.osv.com, where you will also find the PowerPoints for each session. The password to access these resources and the PowerPoints is the 5th word on page 30.

If you are interested in purchasing the pamphlets recommended in each session's Take-Home Resources, visit orderosv.com/product-category/pamphlets.

SMALL-GROUP DISCUSSION GUIDELINES

- Please treat everything shared as being confidential. Your discussion group is like Las Vegas — what is shared in the group stays in the group.
- Stay on topic, and answer the questions provided. Steer clear of current and/or controversial topics that might lead to debate versus sharing.
- Encourage everyone in the group to participate — but require no one to do so.
- Listen and share respectfully. Avoid criticism, judgment, preaching, or teaching.
- Make sure all have time to contribute to the discussion. Avoid dominating the time or interrupting someone else.
- Keep your answers brief so everyone has the opportunity to share.

SMALL-GROUP DISCUSSION GUIDELINES
- Please treat everything shared as being confidential. Your discussion group is like Las Vegas — what is shared in the group stays in the group.
- Stay on topic, and answer the questions provided. Steer clear of current and/or controversial topics that might lead to debate versus sharing.
- Encourage everyone in the group to participate — but require no one to do so.
- Listen and share respectfully. Avoid criticism, judgment, preaching, or teaching.
- Make sure all have time to contribute to the discussion. Avoid dominating the time or interrupting someone else.
- Keep your answers brief so everyone has the opportunity to share.

TODAY'S TAKEAWAY (ALL SESSIONS)

DATE:

Today's Takeaway …

DATE:

Today's Takeaway …

DATE:

Today's Takeaway …

SESSION 1: THE BIG QUESTIONS OF LIFE

Discussion Questions

Do the "My Journey" activity individually first.
Briefly introduce yourself:

Name
Where you are from
Special interests or hobbies

1. Looking at the "My Journey" activity, are there any surprises or new insights about your life that you'd like to share?

2. Have there been times in your life when you experienced God's closeness or absence?

3. Do you/did you feel the presence of God more during the bad times of your life or during the good times?

4. Are there any events that have made you question the meaning of life in general or your life specifically?

5. Can you think of a/the time when you realized that your life had a specific meaning and purpose?

My Journey

- Above the timeline, on a scale of 1 to 5, with 5 being the pinnacle, note the good and joyful times in your life with a *G*: falling in love, getting married, graduating, earning promotions, having a child, and other memorable moments.

- Connect the *G*s from left to right

- Below the timeline, on a scale of 1 to 5, with 5 being the lowest point, note the bad and challenging times in your life with a *B*: death, divorce, illness, job loss, and so on.

- Connect the *B*s from left to right.

- Looking at the "Good Times" line, mark a *C* at points on the line when you felt close to God.

- Looking at the "Bad Times" line, mark a *D* at points on the line when you felt angry with or distant from God. If, however, you felt close to God instead of angry or distant during a bad time, mark that time with a *C*.

- Take a moment to examine your journey and reflect upon its meaning to you.

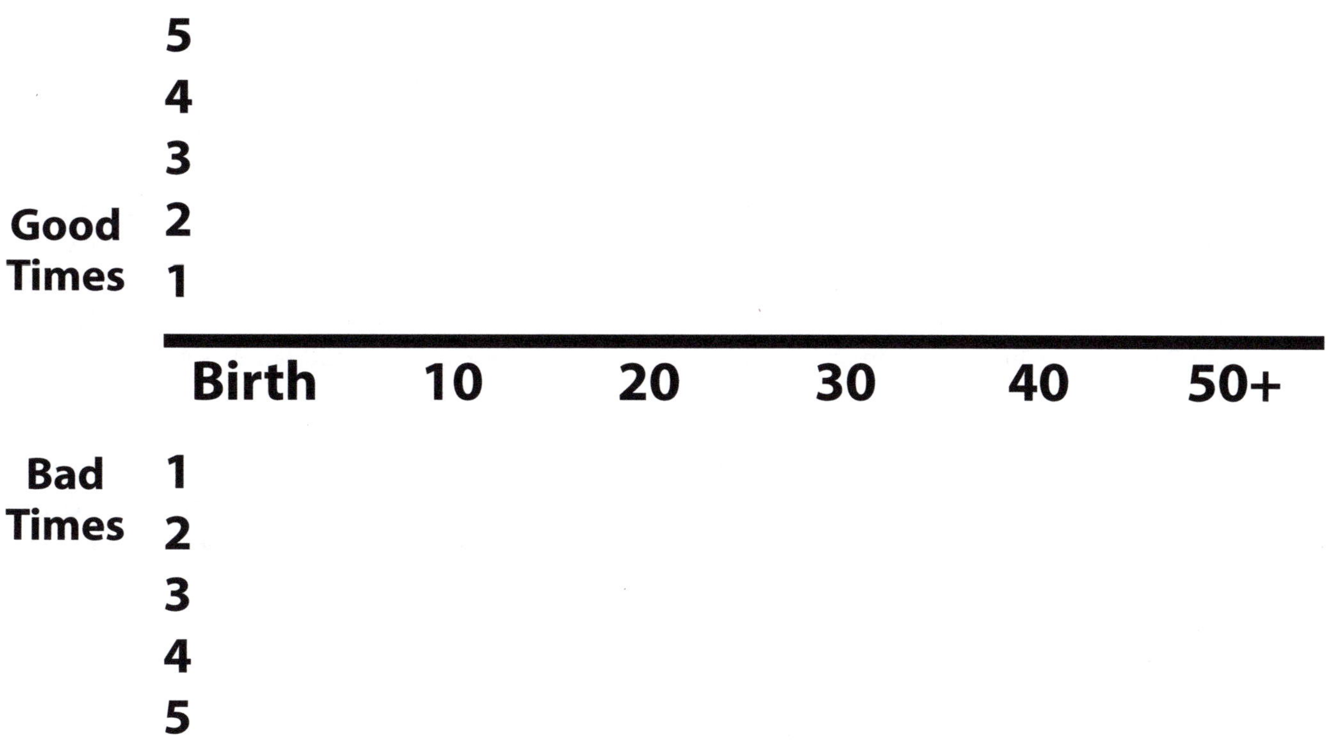

What Catholics Need to Know About Making Their Homes a Domestic Church

Donna-Marie Cooper O'Boyle, *Our Sunday Visitor*, March 21, 2011

The Catholic presence stretches around the globe, and its numbers are increasing worldwide, according to statistics from the 2011 *Annuario Pontificio* ("pontifical yearbook"). Approximately 1.18 billion belong to the big Church, the Body of Christ. In many cases they are also living in one of the countless little "domestic churches" all throughout the world.

But what actually constitutes a "domestic church"? Let's take a quick look at the beginning of the Church's founder's life. Jesus himself was born into the heart of a family, a little domestic church consisting of his mother, Mary; his foster father, St. Joseph; and himself. Wherever the Holy Family set up their home — in the stable in Bethlehem for a time, in Egypt or in Nazareth — their domestic church moved right along with them simply because their domestic church consisted of the three of them.

Down through the ages, as people were converted and became believers, "they desired that 'their whole household' should also be saved. These families who became believers were islands of Christian life in an unbelieving world" (*Catechism of the Catholic Church*, No. 1655).

Building up Church

Just as the early Christian families were an exemplary example to others around them, Catholic families today can build up their own domestic churches and strive to be "islands of Christian life in an unbelieving world."

"Every home is called to become a 'domestic church' in which family life is completely centered on the lordship of Christ and the love of husband and wife mirrors the mystery of Christ's love for the Church, his bride," Pope Benedict XVI said in his February 7, 2007, general audience remarks.

These are wonderful ideals to emulate. However, because of the large number of single-parent families today, we know that not every Catholic family consists of a mother and a father. Broken families seem more like a norm rather than an exception. Grandparents are raising their grandchildren in many households. And we also know that even in traditional families, not every Catholic husband and wife "mirrors the mystery of Christ's love for the Church, his bride." Even so, our Church summons Catholic families, in all their shapes and forms, to live in this virtuous way. Each unique domestic church can be a stable, loving, and holy environment.

A domestic church begins with the Sacrament of Matrimony — man and woman become husband and wife. Pope John Paul II spoke of a Catholic couple's call to holiness within that sacrament when he said, "Marriage is an act of will that signifies and involves a mutual gift, which unites the spouses and binds them to their eventual souls, with whom they make up a sole family — a domestic church."

He also explained the husband and wife's responsibility to recognize and to act upon their role as "givers of life" in his encyclical *Evangelium Vitae* (The Gospel of Life):

"As the domestic church, the family is summoned to proclaim, celebrate, and serve the Gospel of life. This is a responsibility which first concerns married couples, called to be givers of life, on the basis of an ever greater awareness of the meaning of procreation as a unique event which clearly reveals that human life is a gift received in order then to be given as a gift. In giving origin to a new life, parents recognize that the child 'as the fruit of their mutual gift of love, is in turn, a gift for both of them, a gift which flows from them'" (92).

As babies are born and families grow, the parents, considered the first and foremost educators by the Church, are called to pass on the Catholic faith to their children. Mother Teresa explained this experience in the domestic church very simply. She said, "The best and surest way to learn the love of Jesus is through the family."

Curriculum of Love

Catholic parents can look to the *Catechism* for direction regarding their responsibilities to impart the faith to their children. There we learn, "The Christian home is the place where children receive the first proclamation of the faith. For this reason, the family home is rightly called 'the domestic church,' a community of grace and prayer, a school of human virtues and of Christian charity" (1666).

Within the walls of the domestic church, children learn about their faith through their parents' and grandparents' word and example, as well as within the many growing pains and nitty-gritty details of everyday life as a family grows together in holiness.

Everyday life in the family may seem filled with a lot of ordinariness and at times a bit of chaos. Yet, right there along with the normal routines and day-to-day occurrences of sibling rivalry, teenaged angst and sometimes grouchy spouses is woven a paradigm of human enrichment pointing us to a narrow path that leads to heaven.

Catholic teachings open our eyes to the remarkable goings on within a growing faithful Catholic family, helping us recognize that there is a heck of a lot more happening in our day-to-day lives than what meets the eye.

"It is here that the father of the family, the mother, children, and all members of the family exercise the priesthood of the baptized in a privileged way 'by the reception of the sacraments, prayer and thanksgiving, the witness of a holy life, and self-denial and active charity.' Thus the home is the first school of Christian life and 'a school for human enrichment.' Here one learns endurance and the joy of work, fraternal love, generous — even repeated — forgiveness, and above all divine worship in prayer and the offering of one's life" (1657).

Amazing! And we thought we were simply teaching our kids how to share, love, and pray, potty training them, breaking up fights, functioning as lovingly as possible after sleepless nights, laying down the law, and rescuing them from far too many lurking dangers. But, in reality, it is within the domestic church that Catholic parents lay out a curriculum of fraternal love and forgiveness while helping the family to work out their salvation in the give-and-take of life in the family.

A High Calling

Whether we live in a palace or a cave, Catholic parents have the awesome responsibility of raising their children to not only learn right from wrong, but also to recognize that the real purpose of their lives in this world is to work out their salvation for the next world — their eternal lives. This has to be the number one priority in raising Christian children. God provides the blessing of a family structure to accomplish this.

The Church teaches us, "Since parents have conferred life on their children, they have a most solemn obligation to educate their offspring. Hence, parents must be acknowledged as the first and foremost educators of their children. Their role as educators is so decisive that scarcely anything can compensate for their failure in it. For it devolves on parents to create a family atmosphere so animated with love and reverence for God and others that a well-rounded personal and social development will be fostered among children. Hence, the family is the first school of those social virtues which every society needs" (Declaration on Christian Education, *Gravissimum Educationis*, 3).

Parents certainly have a high calling. We also learn from that same document: "The role of parents in education is of such importance that it is almost impossible to provide an adequate substitute."

The *Catechism* tells us, "Parents have the first responsibility for the education of their children. They bear witness to this responsibility first by creating a home where tenderness, forgiveness, respect, fidelity, and disinterested service are the rule. The home is well suited for education in the virtues. This requires an apprenticeship in self-denial, sound judgment and self-mastery — the preconditions of all true freedom. Parents should teach their children to subordinate the 'material and instinctual dimensions to interior and spiritual ones'" (2223).

As first and foremost educator, parents will ultimately be answering to God with regard to how their children have been educated. Yes, that means parents need to investigate all that is going on in their children's education, not just at home, but also in their schools, both Catholic and public, and their religious education programs.

Eyes Toward Heaven

To help pave the way to heaven for the children, it's essential for parents to establish an atmosphere of prayer in the home. They'll first want to ground themselves in prayer, making it an integral part of their daily lives.

If children are raised in a household of prayer, prayer will become as natural as breathing to them and will indeed provide a secure foundation. Kids take cues from their best role models, their parents and grandparents. The example of prayers said in the morning and evening, for special intentions at various times, and at the dinner table speaks volumes since children look to adults and learn their behaviors.

To help our family focus more on the sacred rather than the secular, we must bring something of the big Church into our little domestic church. We do that by placing sacred images around our home. Sacred art, icons, crucifixes, images of the Sacred Heart of Jesus, the Immaculate Heart of Mary, the Holy Family, saints' pictures, sacramentals, holy-water fonts, and even a prayer corner can adorn our homes. These holy items help stir the soul and lift our attention toward heaven and its rewards.

Nourishing Bodies, Souls

Dinnertime is a lot more than just about filling our bellies. It's a time to grow together as a family, creating memories and establishing traditions.

Our dinner conversations may not always be so profound, and our children's behavior may not always be Hallmark picture perfect. Things happen, kids can get messy and loud, and we may lose our patience at times. We are human, after all. A growing family is a work in progress, and parents are wise to lower their expectations with regard to their children's behavior while still teaching them to show respect and practice their manners as best they can. Mealtimes are certainly those occasions when "tenderness, forgiveness, respect, fidelity, and disinterested service are the rule."

Introducing prayer at the dinner table is not only beneficial, it's also essential. Why not use the time wisely? You will have a captive audience, after all. After Grace Before Meals is said, you can add an Our Father, a Hail Mary and any special intentions. In just a few minutes' time, you will have united your family in prayer.

God gives Christian families countless opportunities to earn grace throughout their daily lives within their domestic church as they forge a blessed bond together and help one another come closer to their eternal reward. These families can become a beacon of light in our darkened world.

Donna-Marie Cooper O'Boyle is author of "The Domestic Church: Room by Room" (Servant Books, 2011) and "Grace Café: Serving Up Recipes for Faithful Mothering" (Circle Press, $14.95) and host of EWTN's "Everyday Blessings for Catholic Moms." For more information, visit www.donnacooperoboyle.com.

SESSION 2: THE GOD OF LOVE AND MERCY

Discussion Questions

1. What is your earliest memory of thinking about God?

2. Who taught you that God the Father is the loving father of all creation?

3. Have there been times when have you questioned or doubted God the Father's love and mercy?

4. If God is our loving Father, why do you think he allows us to go through loss and pain?

5. What are some ways you have seen God the Father's love and mercy expressed in your life?

6. Is there someone whom you know personally who has been a living example of the Father's love and mercy?

Teaching Your Child About God

Dr. Marylynn Wesson
(Part 1 in a series of 3)

The thought of having a discussion or teaching your child about God often strikes fear in the heart of a parent. It can seem daunting, especially if you don't fully understand who God is or if you feel that you can't adequately verbalize what you do understand. You needn't be intimidated, as talking to children about God is surprisingly simple. Here are six suggestions:

1. **Remember how your child sees the world in their earliest years and tap into that.** Children have an inborn sense of awe and wonder that can be easily nurtured. Whenever they have a bad day, a scary thought, or a nightmare, that is an opportunity to share with them the protective love of God who watches over them and cares about their fears and struggles. Snuggle up with them and help them visualize God holding them protectively as they sleep, play, go to school, etc.

2. Another opportunity to tap into their way of viewing the world is to **focus on the beauty of creation, attributing the creation of that beauty to God**. You might even say a quick prayer of gratitude: "Thank you, God, for ____." Nothing fancy is required, and children don't need much prompting (or discussion) to understand, as this type of observation is natural for them. As a toddler, my son would grab my hand and say, "Come, Mommy, let's go look at the 'myoon.'" We would go outside and marvel at the beauty of the moon. Those moments are some of my fondest memories of his childhood and are also some of the moments when I felt closest to God.

3. It's also helpful in teaching children about God to **be careful about what media they see and hear**. Listen to a Christian music station or find a suitable playlist. There are several on Spotify, including "Catholic Kids Worship Radio" and "Catholic Songs for Kids." Music is mighty, and children love and learn from it more than we may realize, especially before they can read. When allowing screen time, along with pure entertainment, include some Bible story videos. My young son was particularly fond of the story of David and Goliath because of the "good guy versus bad guy" theme as well as the fact that David was small. He identified with it because — as he was little at the time — the little guy was the superhero of the story.

4. **Be aware that, just like your own faith journey, a child learning about God is a process that plays out over time.** When children first ask questions, they initially will likely be simple ones that only require simple responses. Explaining God doesn't mean you need to have great knowledge of theological concepts. Rather, speak from your heart and share simply and plainly, addressing only the question asked rather than launching into a deeper explanation. There is no need to address something that they are not asking.

5. **If your child asks a question about God that you don't know how to answer, don't panic.** It's all right to admit that you don't know everything about God, but you can find the answers. You don't know everything about how to make your children well when they are sick either, but you do know where to take them to see someone who does.

6. Children ask sincere — and sometimes difficult — questions that deserve truthful answers. This is especially true as children grow older and become more aware of the perplexities of life. So **admit that you don't know the answer to their question, but tell them you will find the answer together.** Work with their natural curiosity and go on an information hunt with them; the time spent doing so will be well spent. Good first sources for information are the Bible and the *Catechism of the Catholic Church*. Other trusted sources would include your pastor, director of religious education, the United States Conference of Catholic Bishops website, FORMED (if your parish has it), Our Sunday Visitor, and Catholic Answers.

Teaching Your Child About God, continued

7. Pray with your child. Keep it simple and conversational, teaching your child to talk to God just as they would a friend. Teach them to pray before meals, when they are happy or sad about something, upon rising (a simple "Good morning God! Thank you for a good night's sleep!" will do), and at bedtime, where they pray for others and tell God about their day. Doing this daily will then become a natural routine and will lay the foundation for a child to understand that God is their friend. You might consider having a special prayer area or altar that displays religious items. A Bible, crucifix, rosary, religious art, a statue of the Blessed Virgin Mary, etc., are wonderful reminders of your family's professed beliefs.

8. Teach your child about God by teaching with your life. Over time, children are more likely to do what you do rather than listen to what you say. If you want your child to grow up with a love and reverence for God, it is critical to model for them that which you want them to understand. You must teach with your life because you are the first and most influential teacher that your child will have. In that role, through your words and deeds, you teach your child about God's love and mercy by the way you treat others and forgive transgressions. When you make a mistake, acknowledge it, apologize, and ask for forgiveness.

9. The most important way to teach your child with your life is to attend Mass every Sunday. Deliberately or neglectfully missing Mass is a serious sin, as the Church teaches: "The Sunday Eucharist is the foundation and confirmation of all Christian practice. For this reason, the faithful are obliged to participate in the Eucharist on days of obligation, unless excused for a serious reason (for example, illness, the care of infants) or dispensed by their own pastor. Those who deliberately fail in this obligation commit a grave sin" (CCC 2181).

10. Remember what Saint Luke the Evangelist recorded Jesus saying about children and faith: "But Jesus called for them and said, 'Let the little children come to me, and do not stop them; for it is to such as these that the kingdom of God belongs. Truly I tell you, whoever does not receive the kingdom of God as a little child will never enter it" (Lk 18:16–17). The point that Jesus is making is that knowing and receiving God's message and will for our lives does not involve great knowledge or theological training but, rather, trust — just like the trust of a young child. They often understand God better than adults. So fear not, relax, and enjoy this moment in your child's spiritual awakening and journey.

SESSION 3: WHO DO YOU SAY THAT I AM?

Discussion Questions

1. Who is Jesus to you?

2. Describe something about Jesus' story with which you identify.

3. Do you feel close to Jesus? In what ways?

4. In what ways might you fear experiencing closeness with Jesus — fear developing a close, personal, and intimate relationship with him?

5. Describe a teaching of Jesus that makes following him and being his disciple difficult.

6. Thinking about the significance of Jesus' resurrection, what do you need to stop putting ahead of your relationship with him?

Teaching Your Child About Jesus

Dr. Marylynn Wesson
(Part 2 in a series of 3)

One of the most important — if not the most important — things you'll do as a parent is to introduce your child to Jesus. The first step is for you to have a relationship with him yourself. To nurture your relationship, make sure to spend time with him and closely follow him. When you do so, you'll find that talking to your child about Jesus becomes easy and natural.

You want your child to develop an understanding of Jesus and come to know him because of what's at stake.

In the Gospel of John, Jesus says, "I am the way, and the truth, and the life. No one comes to the Father except through me" (14:6). What Jesus is saying is that he is the "gate" to heaven — the bridge to eternal life. What this means for us who are baptized is significant. For the baptized, salvation consists in a union with Jesus that begins at baptism, is nurtured through the sacraments and a personal relationship with Jesus, and culminates in union with God forever in heaven after we die, if we have not rejected that relationship with Jesus through serious sin at the time of our death.

Jesus is the only way to the Father and the only Mediator between heaven and earth. It's his responsibility to discern the state of someone's soul and their salvation. Our sole responsibility is to live and share Jesus' gospel message with others — especially with our children.

Your child's faith will best develop into a mature, salvific faith if they learn to follow Jesus from a young age. The only way for them to learn to follow is to be taught about him so that they can say "yes" to Jesus all their life. One of the best ways to introduce children to Jesus initially is to read to them colorfully illustrated children's Bible story books that tell the story of Jesus' life. Short stories and colorful pictures capture the attention and imagination of a young child. Plus, most children love nothing more than curling up with a parent and being read to. Both of my children enjoyed being read to well beyond the age when they were able to read themselves. Most children also love watching videos, and several resources are available online. Introducing your child to Jesus in these ways should prompt questions on their part and give you the opportunity to answer in an age-appropriate way. Their questions will probably be simple, so keep your answers simple.

One interesting observation I've made about children is that they are like sponges who are ready to soak up the stories and truths of our faith. We have so many naturally occurring opportunities to teach children about the goodness and greatness of God and Jesus' gospel message. Remain aware and alert for such teachable moments. Faith development is a process, and the story of Jesus is one of the best ways for children to identify with their Savior as they begin their faith journey by following him. Some suggestions for how to do that are as follows:

1. Begin by introducing them to the story of Jesus as an infant and child. Talk about where he was born, when and where he lived, his family, and the fact that he ate, slept, played, cried when he skinned his knees, and laughed at funny things. In fact, while he was a child and growing up, Jesus had experiences just like our children have.

2. Introduce the topic of sin by explaining that sin interferes with the loving relationship that our great and good God wants to have with everyone. Further explain that sin also disrupts peaceful and loving relationships between people. Point out that one of the reasons God sent Jesus from heaven was so he could experience what it means to be human and then show us all how to live our lives. From Jesus' story, children can learn what he taught about God's unconditional love, abundant mercy, and unceasing forgiveness. For a child to believe that Jesus is who the Bible says he is, come to faith, and seek a personal relationship with him, they need to understand sin and the need for our Savior.

3. Particularly with older children, don't be afraid to talk about death. Specifically, talk with them about how Jesus came to earth to show us that he loved us so much — and how he willingly went to his death on the

Teaching Your Child About Jesus, continued

cross to redeem everyone from sin, thereby opening the door to the hope of eternal life. He conquered the evil of death with his resurrection. He proved that there is, indeed, a life after bodily death. Jesus' resurrection is the "crowning truth" (*Catechism of the Catholic Church*, 638). The Resurrection matters — without it, Christianity would have no meaning.

4. Attend Mass every Sunday with your child. As baptized persons, we are called to participate in Mass on Sundays and other holy days of obligation. Deliberately or neglectfully missing Mass is a serious sin. When children attend Mass regularly, they are more properly disposed to understand the significance of their preparation to receive the Lord's Body, Blood, Soul, and Divinity in the Eucharist for the first time. The Eucharist is the primary means to encounter Jesus, in a way that keeps us alive spiritually so that we might forever enjoy his company in heaven. Therefore, the importance of regular Mass attendance for your child's sake cannot be stressed enough. The example you set is the greatest impetus for children in keeping the Faith. As the parent whom God provided to your child, you are the person tasked with building your child's firm foundation of faith by teaching about him and leading them to him. Without a strong foundation, they will find it hard to survive the challenges of life with their faith and souls intact. Your example can lead your child away from Jesus — or to him.

SESSION 4: THE COMFORTER
Scripture Verses

When the Spirit of truth comes, he will guide you into all the truth; for he will not speak on his own, but will speak whatever he hears, and he will declare to you the things that are to come. (John 16:13)

• • •

But you will receive power when the Holy Spirit has come upon you; and you will be my witnesses in Jerusalem, in all Judea and Samaria, and to the end of the earth. (Acts of the Apostles 1:8)

• • •

Day by day, as they spent much time together in the temple, they broke bread at home[a] and ate their food with glad and generous hearts, praising God and having the goodwill of all the people. And day by day the Lord added to their number those who were being saved. (Acts of the Apostles 2:46–47)

• • •

And hope does not disappoint us, because God's love has been poured into our hearts through the Holy Spirit that has been given to us. (Romans 5:5)

• • •

Likewise the Spirit helps us in our weakness; for we do not know how to pray as we ought, but that very Spirit intercedes with sighs too deep for words. (Romans 8:26)

SESSION 4: THE COMFORTER

Discussion Questions

1. One of the primary works of the Holy Spirit is to pour out God's love into your heart. When have you experienced feeling the love of God?

2. When have you experienced the Holy Spirit at work in your life?

3. Who in your life was or is filled with the Holy Spirit?

4. The gifts of the Holy Spirit are as follows:

    - Wisdom
    - Understanding
    - Counsel
    - Knowledge
    - Piety
    - Fortitude
    - Fear of the Lord

Which do you think are your strongest gifts?

1. The fruits of the Holy Spirit are as follows:

    - Kindness
    - Generosity
    - Joy
    - Charity
    - Self-control
    - Faithfulness
    - Gentleness
    - Goodness
    - Chastity
    - Peace
    - Patience
    - Modesty

Which fruit do you see most in your life? Which one would you like to see more of?

Teaching Your Child About the Holy Spirit

Marylynn Wesson, D. Min.
(Part 3 in a series of 3)

We can't talk about the Holy Spirit without first talking about the Trinity. But the Trinity is a difficult concept for most adults to understand. So teaching a child about the third Person in the Trinity may seem impossible. However, children might be better able to understand, receive, and accept the mystery of the Trinity, because they comprehend and easily accept that there's more to life than the physical reality in which we live.

The Trinity is the mystery of one God in three Persons: God the Father, God the Son, and God the Holy Spirit. The *Catechism of the Catholic Church* explains that "the divine persons do not share the one divinity among themselves but each of them is God whole and entire" (253).

The Holy Spirit is "the Lord, the giver of life, who proceeds from the Father and the Son, who with the Father and the Son is adored and glorified," as we recite in the Nicene Creed.

When we are baptized, the rite of baptism invokes all three Persons of the Trinity. Through the grace of the Sacrament of Baptism, we become members of the Body of Christ, receive the Holy Spirit, and are made adopted sons and daughters of God (CCC 1265) in a spiritual sense. The Father created us, the Son redeemed us, and the Holy Spirit comes to dwell inside us. This divine reality gives us the capacity to believe in God, grow in virtue, and live and act under the prompting of the Holy Spirit (1266). The Sacrament of Confirmation is necessary to complete the grace we received at baptism; in this sacrament, the confirmandi receive a "special strength of the Holy Spirit" to be able to be true witnesses of Christ through actions and words (1285).

The image of a shamrock illustrates the Trinity in a unique way; its symbolism is an effective way to explain the Trinity to anyone — not just children. Legend has it that Saint Patrick used the three-leafed shamrock to explain the Holy Trinity to the fifth-century pagan Irish by explaining that the three persons of God were one, like the three separate leaf points are part of one clover.

The image below is one that older children and adults will understand as illustrating deeper theological concepts of the Trinity. It describes in detail how the three persons of the Trinity are distinct from one another — yet are all one God.

The Holy Spirit proceeds from the Father and the

Teaching Your Child About the Holy Spirit, continued

Son and is the love that exists between them. The Holy Spirit's purpose is to be sent to dwell in God's children upon baptism, directing and guiding anyone who listens to the "still small voice" of his presence within.

Teaching children the purpose of the Holy Spirit as their lifelong helper, teacher, comforter, and friend will help them learn to listen to the Holy Spirit as they grow. They need to know that the Holy Spirit lives within them — that he helps them know and understand God's love and feel his presence in their life, teaches them right from wrong, and comforts them when they are sad. The Holy Spirit is their ever-present best friend.

As parents and guardians, we are called to set a lifelong example of praying and being open to the graces and gifts of the Holy Spirit so that our children will do the same. Families who pray together teach our children that their true strength is drawn from God through the power of his Spirit, whom they can count on to give them what they need to persevere in this life. And if allowed, the Holy Spirit will direct, guide, and lead them to follow Jesus into eternal life.

SESSION 5: THE GOOD NEWS

Discussion Questions

1. What is your earliest memory of hearing Scripture read? Who was reading it, and where?

2. Were Bible stories read to you as a child? If so, who was reading the Bible stories to you?

3. What is your favorite Bible story?

4. What significant person in your childhood read the Bible regularly?

5. Have you ever been involved in a Bible study?

    - If yes, what was your takeaway? What did you learn that you didn't already know?

    - If no, what has prevented you from studying the word of God?

6. Before this class, did you know what the "Good News" was?

7. What are your thoughts about the Good News — the story of Jesus' life, sacrifice, death, and resurrection — and what it means for a relationship with God?

BIBLE BOOKSHELF

SESSION 6: FAITH AND COMMUNITY

Discussion Questions

1. What do you think about the importance of being part of a faith community?

2. What do you think are the differences between believing, knowing about, and following Jesus?

3. What does it mean to you to follow Christ?

4. Do you think that it is possible to believe and know about him but not follow him? Why or why not?

5. What are your thoughts when you hear someone say, "I'm spiritual but not religious"?

6. What do you think are the benefits of having friends-in-Christ?

7. Have you actively sought friendships with those who share your faith beliefs? Why or why not?

SESSION 7: THE POWER OF PRAYER

Discussion Questions

1. What are your greatest obstacles to private prayer?

2. When you pray, what distracts you from prayer the most?

3. On a day-to-day basis, how do you stay in touch with God?

4. Share a specific way that God has answered your prayers.

5. When have you felt that God has let you down?

6. Does submitting yourself to God in prayer — praying for his will in your life — make you anxious or feel too vulnerable? Why or why not?

7. How would you explain the power of prayer — or why it is important to pray — to someone who might not pray?

Basic Catholic Prayers

The Sign of the Cross

In the name of the Father, and of the Son, and of the Holy Spirit. Amen.

• • •

Our Father

Our Father, who art in heaven, hallowed be thy name; thy kingdom come, thy will be done, on earth as it is in heaven. Give us this day our daily bread and forgive us our trespasses, as we forgive those who trespass against us, and lead us not into temptation, but deliver us from evil. Amen.

• • •

Jesus Prayer

Lord Jesus Christ, Son of God, have mercy on me, a sinner. Amen.

• • •

Come, Holy Spirit

Come, Holy Spirit, fill the hearts of your faithful and enkindle in them the fire of your love. Send forth your Spirit, and they shall be created. And you shall renew the face of the earth. Let us pray, O God, who has taught the hearts of the faithful by the light of the Holy Spirit, grant that by the gift of the same Spirit we may be always truly wise and ever rejoice in his consolation, through Christ our Lord. Amen.

• • •

Glory Be (Doxology)

Glory be to the Father, and to the Son, and to the Holy Spirit. As it was in the beginning, is now, and ever shall be, world without end. Amen.

• • •

Hail Mary

Hail Mary, full of grace, the Lord is with thee. Blessed art thou among women, and blessed is the fruit of thy womb, Jesus. Holy Mary, mother of God, pray for us sinners now and at the hour of our death. Amen.

• • •

Basic Catholic Prayers, continued

Apostles' Creed

I believe in God, the Father almighty, creator of heaven and earth, and in Jesus Christ, his only Son, our Lord, who was conceived by the Holy Spirit, born of the Virgin Mary, suffered under Pontius Pilate, was crucified, died, and was buried. He descended into hell; the third day he rose again from the dead; he ascended into heaven and is seated at the right hand of the Father; from thence he shall come to judge the living and the dead. I believe in the Holy Spirit, the holy Catholic Church, the communion of saints, the forgiveness of sins, the resurrection of the body, and life everlasting. Amen.

• • •

The Nicene Creed

We believe in one God, the Father, the Almighty, Maker of all that is, seen and unseen. We believe in one Lord, Jesus Christ, the only Son of God, eternally begotten of the Father, God from God, Light from Light, true God from true God, begotten, not made, consubstantial of one Being with the Father. Through him all things were made. For us men and for our salvation he came down from heaven, and by the Holy Spirit was incarnate of the Virgin Mary, and became man. For our sake he was crucified under Pontius Pilate; he suffered death and was buried. On the third day he rose again in accordance with the Scriptures; he ascended into heaven and is seated at the right hand of the Father. He will come again in glory to judge the living and the dead, and his kingdom will have no end. We believe in the Holy Spirit, the Lord, the giver of life, who proceeds from the Father and the Son. With the Father and the Son he is worshiped and glorified. He has spoken through the Prophets. We believe in one holy catholic and apostolic Church. We acknowledge one baptism for the forgiveness of sins. We look for the resurrection of the dead, and the life of the world to come. Amen.

• • •

Prayer Before Meals

Bless us, O Lord, and these thy gifts, which we are about to receive, from thy bounty, through Christ, our Lord. Amen.

• • •

Prayer to Our Guardian Angel

Angel of God, my guardian dear, to whom God's love commits me here, ever this day be at my side to light and guard, to rule and guide. Amen.

• • •

Act of Contrition (Prayer of the Penitent)

My God, I am sorry for my sins with all my heart. In choosing to do wrong and failing to do good, I have sinned against you whom I should love above all things. I firmly intend, with your help to do penance, to sin no more, and to avoid whatever leads me to sin. Our Savior Jesus Christ suffered and died for us. In his name, my God, have mercy. Amen.

SESSION 8: LISTENING TO THAT STILL, SMALL VOICE

Discussion Questions

1. How do you feel about your prayer life?

2. What process do you follow when it comes to making big decisions?

3. What other voices, besides God's, influence your decisions?

4. What needs or attachments prevent you from seeking and following God's will over your own will or the will of others?

5. What advice would you give others who are making a difficult decision?

6. When have you experienced hearing God's voice?

7. How could you discern that this was God speaking to you and not something or someone else?